Klas Sand.. .f Östman

Education for Sustainable Development

Nature, School and Democracy

Translation: Roger Billingham

 Studentlitteratur

Swedish title: Miljödidaktik. Naturen, skolan och demokratin
Published by Studentlitteratur 2003
© The Authors and Studentlitteratur 2003

 Copying prohibited

The papers and inks used in this product
are eco-friendly.

Art. No 31610
ISBN 978-91-44-03377-8
Edition 1:5

© The Authors and Studentlitteratur 2005
www.studentlitteratur.se

Translation: Roger Billingham
Illustrations by Margareta Lindman
Cover design by Francisco Ortega

Printed by Holmbergs i Malmö AB, Sweden 2008

Contents

Part II   Perspectives on Current Environmental
          Problems

Part III Teaching and Learning Perspectives on ESD

Preface

Certain tasks in life have a sense of urgency in comparison with others; one of those is writing a book that can contribute towards encouraging teachers and future teachers to assume a deeper sense of commitment towards the environment and sustainable development. As the 2003 Swedish edition of this book was well received it has been possible for us to update and translate it into English, which we feel is a vitally important step in the international work being carried out on these issues, especially since the UN has declared 2005–2015 to be the decade of Education for Sustainable Development.

We have reason to thank a great number of people and institutions for their inspiration, points of view and support in making this book possible. We would, however, particularly like to thank our translator Roger Billingham (who also translated all the original quotations) – many thanks! – and our dedicated reference staff whose knowledge, competence and experience within the subjects addressed in this book has been indispensable: Göran Bostedt, Peter Fredman, Eva Friman, Maria Frisk, Knut Per Hasund, Staffan Hellstrand, David Kronlid, Lars J. Lundgren, Niclas Månsson, Christer Nordlund, Sverre Sjölander, Per Wickenberg, Per-Olof Wickman and Anders Öckerman. We would also like to thank some of the most important financing sources which have represented a necessary base for our research work: the Swedish Council for Planning and Coordination of Research, The Swedish Research Council, The Mountain Mistra Programme, the Swedish National Agency of Education, and the Swedish National Agency for School Improvement.

Klas Sandell,   *Johan Öhman*   *and Leif Östman*

Äskholm   Örebro   Västeråker

Introduction: Teaching Competence in Education for Sustainable Development

The Shift from Environmental Education to Education for Sustainable Development

In recent years the discussions on environmental education have been focusing to a large extent on a possible shift from environmental education (EE) to education for sustainable development (ESD).[1]

Traditionally, environmental education was based on the belief that certain sets of values, knowledge-perspectives and attitudes are better able to contribute to environmental friendly action and the solving of environmental problems than others. These principles should, therefore, be prioritised in environmental education. Accordingly, it was the task of environmental educators to formulate certain standards of environmental education and to develop both content and methods that modify the behaviour of students in accordance with those values and perspectives.

In the contemporary debate, however, most authors emphasise the social and cultural context-dependent character of the issues concerning environmental and developmental problems. This perspective has given rise to several approaches on environmental education that are less openly normative than the traditional methods. A point of departure for these approaches is that there are many conflicting voices about environmental questions in democratic societies and that nobody is in a neutral position to decide upon what actions will be most beneficial for our environment in the future. It has therefore been stressed that environmental education

---

1   At the end of this introduction there is a list of books and articles discussing environmental education and education for sustainable development.

should be characterised by *pluralism*. An important standpoint among these approaches is that re-establishing the essential role of education will support the freedom to form one's own opinion and enhancing students' competence in participating in a democratic debate. There are however also those pointing at the risk that such a pluralistic approach leads to the opinion that all the ecological limitations for life on earth are social constructions and therefore negotiable, and that the seriousness of the environmental crisis in this way is neglected.

Many authors and researchers have brought attention to the potential of ESD in this change towards a more pluralistic approach. As they see it, ESD creates the opportunity to make a new start and re-orient and vitalise environmental education. It is made clear here that there can never be a fixed connection between sustainability and development, hence the concept of ESD must be formed in relation to the local cultural, geographical, social and historical circumstances in which the education is to be put into practice. From this point of view ESD broadens the scope of EE as it connects ecological, economic and social development and thus creates a balance between sustainable human development and environmental protection. These authors maintain that ESD can be regarded as a tool in the achievement of sustainability through democratic practice.

But the concept of ESD is not uncontroversial. To some debaters ESD actually opposes pluralism in environmental education. It is pointed out that the policy documents that form the basis of ESD focus exclusively on the well-being of humans and ignore the intrinsic values of nature. In addition, and especially when associated with an economic market philosophy, the concept of 'development' implies a constant economic and technological growth in line with 'more is always better'. Some commentators claim, that in the rhetoric of ESD, education is regarded as a tool for sustainable development, which makes education instrumental in striving for something external to itself and prescribing a preferred end. Thus, ESD is seen as a top-down concept, promoting a specific ideology created by politicians and experts in power, at the cost of the emancipated qualities and the critical dimensions of education.

In this book we are trying to present a *pluralistic view* of ESD, connecting ESD to the important role of education in general to support the *democratic development of society.* In doing this we have tried to keep in mind both the important aspects of EE and the reminders of the problems of ESD as highlighted by its critics.

Requirements for Teaching Sustainable Development

The aim of this book is to contribute to improving teaching competence in the area of sustainable development. How, then, does one define such teaching competence? One way of creating an understanding of what teaching competence involves is to consider the types of problem that a teacher might face when teaching. One type of problem is that which arises in all teaching situations and is formulated in the question: *How shall I deal with this?* Such a question can arise when a student says, "I don't understand". In these situations there is rarely time to reflect – an immediate response is required. When we respond we must take into consideration a number of specific factors, such as who is asking the question, the level that he/she is at, the type of difficulties they usually encounter and whether similar areas have already been covered etc. It is not possible to learn these skills from a book. The answer to the above question is specific to the situation in which it arose. The answer is dependent on the fact that the student, class and teacher are all familiar with each other. It can be said that the answer to the question is, to a large extent, based on practical skills. Practical skills enable the teacher to e.g. individualise the teaching – to ensure that that all the students, depending on their own abilities and backgrounds, are offered the optimum conditions for learning. This knowledge is based on the results of tried and tested teaching skills that develop through practicing the profession for a long period. It can be likened to the way in the skills of a craftsman or craftswoman increase as they become more familiar with their material and tools.

The other type of question – and the one primarily dealt with in this book – concerns the time we have to reflect and consider the situation: *What are my alternatives?* This question does not require an immediate answer, and is more dependent on the reasons for our decision. The answer to the question has a general nature and has therefore a theoretical aspect. In this case theoretical answers or theoretical knowledge can be of help. Theoretical knowledge makes it possible to consider a phenomenon or an event from different perspectives; it is possible to illustrate a problem or a situation based on general reference points. The illustration below demonstrates how the same phenomenon (a cylinder) can be interpreted in two different ways – either as a circle or as a rectangle – dependent on which points of departure are applied in the approach.

Similarly students' difficulties in understanding an aspect of the issues treated in education can be regarded in the same way (e.g. a constructivist teaching theory as opposed to a sociocultural perspective towards teaching). Each perspective will offer a different explanation as to why the students are having difficulty in understanding, just as any potential measures in facilitating their understanding will differ according to which perspective is preferred. A teacher with a lot of theoretical knowledge about teaching and education can consciously adapt the teaching so that the process is made easier for the students.

But not only the learning process of the students can be put into different perspectives, even the teaching content can be highlighted from different starting points. Thus in education, environmental- and developmental issues can be put into several different perspectives (e.g. an ecological, ethical, economical and a political perspective). With each starting point there is a different way to

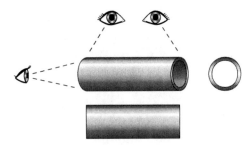

Figure Introduction: 1. Schematic diagram illustrating how the same phenomenon can be described differently from different perspectives.

understand and define how environmental problems occur and how best to solve them. This ability to be able to put environmental and development issues into perspective implies that the teacher e.g. can structure the teaching materials and lessons in a logical way which best allows the students to adopt a critical approach to the subject – skills in discussing environmental and developmental issues from various perspectives – in addition to making conscious evaluations of the different perspectives.

In brief this implies that a teacher with the necessary competence to teach the subject of sustainable development has:

- knowledge of environmental problems and sustainable development,
- theoretical knowledge of teaching and learning,
- practical knowledge and teaching skills (experience).

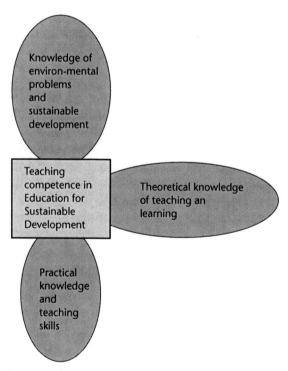

Figure Introduction: 2. Diagram showing the fundamental components of teaching competence in education for sustainable development (ESD).

When both knowledge and skills are integrated, the ability to put environmental- and developmental issues into perspective is developed. In this way they can be presented in lesson form, as well as help to solve problems and facilitate situations within the specific teaching situation.

The aim of this book, then, is to contribute to the advancement of the necessary skills required in order to teach the subject of sustainable development. This includes developing the ability of both active teachers and student teachers to make conscious choices from the alternatives available in the teaching materials and methods in such a way as to expand and deepen students' perspectives on sustainable development.

Book Layout

Apart from this introduction, this book consists of three parts and a conclusion.

Part I

The main point of departure for this book is that the basis for sustainable development lies in humankind's relationship with the natural world. Part I presents a general historical background to humankind's approach to and interaction with the natural world. Here we look at the history of humankind from the hunter-gatherer period up to today's industrial societies with their characteristic environmental problems and with a particular focus on how current environmental commitment has evolved, transformed and intensified over the years. Part I of the book can be described as resting in the encounter between geography, human ecology and environmental history.

Part II

In Part II of the book we take the background and situations from Part I and focus on four current – although principally different – ways of problematising and putting environmental- and development issues into perspective, namely:

- an ecological perspective on what characterises the natural world (chapter four),
- an environmentally ethical perspective on the different ways of morally relating to the natural world (chapter five),
- a political perspective on society's potential methods of dealing with environmental issues (chapter six),
- an economical perspective applied as a means of achieving sustainable development (chapter seven).

The purpose of these points is to bring to the fore four principally different lines of discussion. In addition to highlighting these four methods of problematizing and putting environmental- and development issues into perspective, the chapters also follow a sequence. We begin by considering environmental issues as a question of knowledge; the following chapter then considers the problems from a wider angle by introducing an environmentally ethical perspective. This ensures that the issues cannot be reduced to questions that only address individual knowledge or access to information, and allows the norms and values of individuals to be included in the discussion. Following that we address the questions from a political and democratic perspective, which means that in addition to including the environmentally ethical standpoints of individuals, the questions also encompass deliberations on the possibilities of reaching collective agreements within the democratic social system. Finally, the economic aspect is considered as an example of efforts, based on a certain scientific perspective, to support and implement political decisions related to sustainable development.

Part III

In the third and final part of the book, the education perspective is presented, which highlights the fact that the way in which we relate to environmental- and developmental issues – from the points of view of knowledge, environmental ethics and politics – is something which we learn. In other words, the way we relate to the natural world and social development, as both individuals and members of society, can be directly linked to the way we are educated. In Part III, the aim is to explain how this learning process can be understood and, based on that understanding, present a number of applications and models that can be used in all areas of the teaching process. In chapter eight there is an introductory comparison between education for sustainable development (ESD) and other traditions within environmental education. Chapter nine presents an illustration of the views of the democratic role of education and the consequences of these views within the various traditions of environmental education. In chapters ten, eleven and twelve, the implications of ESD receive particular focus. Chapter ten takes a learning perspective on ESD, where the relationship between the learning of knowledge and the learning of values is one of the subjects addressed. Chapter eleven discusses the teaching perspectives of ESD based on the choices made available to the teacher. In chapter twelve, a closer look is taken, at the practical implications of ESD, with the help of examples.

Conclusion

The book concludes with a discussion about how knowledge and teaching skills in ESD can be developed. The conclusion can also be read as a summary of the book's layout. Additionally we present an outline of the central knowledge requirements of environmental and sustainable development as well as the knowledge on ESD presented in the book.

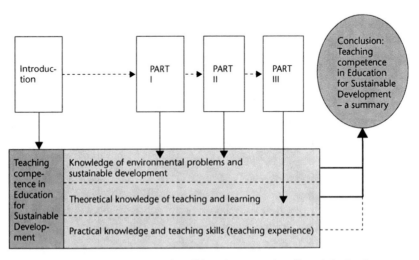

Figure Introduction: 3. Diagram describing the general outline of the book.

Note to Readers

As has already been mentioned, the main aim of the book is to assist in the development of teaching competence in ESD. As the book does not specifically adhere itself to any particular academic subject, and the content stretches over many different fields of sciences, we hope that the reader will have the opportunity to discuss the issues of this book with peers competent in subjects other than his or her own. In such discussions those competent in, for instance, the social sciences can add their insight in sociological perspectives, while others educated in the natural sciences can contribute with their knowledge of ecology etc. We would also like to remind readers that any teaching skills will remain incomplete without the addition of tried and tested experience, and we therefore assume that the book's content will be both consolidated and discussed on the basis of actual experiences of teaching the subject of the environment and sustainable development.

The book layout indicates that while more common environmental problems such as the climate, genetics, energy, biological diversity and the natural landscape, will be brought up as examples, they will not be addressed systematically. The idea is that, due to its structure, the book will encourage discussions on the subject of ESD in Part III. The literature references appear as both footnotes and comments. Each chapter concludes with further details on any references given as well a section for recommended reading.

Further Reading

The following books and articles are recommended for further studies of the discussions on environmental education and education for sustainable development.

Elliott, John (1999). Sustainable Society and Environmental Education: future perspectives and demands for the educational system. *Cambridge Journal of Education*, No. 3, pp. 325–341.

Fien, John (1995). Teaching for a Sustainable World: the environmental and developmental education project for teacher education. *Environmental Education Research*, No. 1, pp. 21–34.

Gough, Stephen (2002). Increasing the Value of the Environment: a 'real options' metaphor for learning. *Environmental Education Research,* No. 1, pp. 61–72.

Huckle, John (1999). Locating Environmental Education Between Modern Capitalism and Postmodern Socialism: A Reply to Lucie Sauvé. *Canadian Journal of Environmental Education,* No. 4, pp. 36–45.

Jensen, Bjarne Bruun; Schnack, Karsten & Simovska, Venka (Eds.) (2000). *Critical Environmental and Health Education: Research Issues and Challenges.* Copenhagen: Research Centre for Environmental and Health Education, The Danish University of Education.

Jensen, Bjarne Bruun & Schnack, Karsten (1997). The Action Competence Approach in Environmental Education. *Environmental Education Research,* No. 3, pp. 163–179.

Jickling, Bob (2003). Environmental Education and Environmental Advocacy: Revisited. *Journal of Environmental Education,* No. 2, pp. 20–27.

Jickling, Bob & Spork, Helen (1998). Education for the Environment: a critique. *Environmental Education Research,* No. 3, pp. 309–328.

Lijmbach, Susanne; Margadant-van Arcken, Marjan; van Koppen, C. S. A. & Wals, Arjen E. J. (2002). 'Your View of Nature is Not Mine': learning about pluralism in the classroom. *Environmental Education Research,* No. 2, pp. 121–135.

Mckeown, Rosalyn & Hopkins, Charles (2003). EE ≠ ESD: defusing the worry. *Environmental Education Research,* No. 1, pp. 117–128.

Rauch, Franz (2002). The Potential of Education for Sustainable Development for Reform in Schools. *Environmental Education Research,* No. 1, pp. 43–51.

Sauvé, Lucie (1999). Environmental Education Between Modernity and Postmodernity: Searching for an Integrating Educational Framework. *Canadian Journal of Environmental Education,* No. 4, pp. 9–36.

Scott, William & Gough, Stephen (Eds.) (2004). *Key Issues in Sustainable Development and Learning: a critical review.* London & New York, RoutledgeFalmer.

Stables, Andrew (2001). Language and Meaning in Environmental Education: an overview. *Environmental Education Research,* No. 2, pp. 121–128.

Stables, Andrew & Scott, William (2002). The Quest for Holism in Education for Sustainable Development. *Environmental Education Research,* No 1, pp. 53–60.

Sterling, Stephen (2001). *Sustainable Education: Re-visioning Learning and Change.* Foxhole, Dartington, Totnes, Devon: Green Books.

Part I
A Background: Environmental
History and Human Ecology

The first part of the book approaches the development of mankind from having been an animal among others to our present state of being able to influence, on a large scale, our own environment and that of others. Chapter one gives an overview of the history of mankind and its main epochs: from hunter-gatherers to the agricultural age and up to today's industrialised society. A couple of more general ideas concerning a possible post-industrial society; on the concept of nature and on mankind's energy sources are also put forward here. In chapter two we follow the rise of modern environmental concerns in parallel with industrialism and the modernisation of society – from the early ideas of nature preservation around the turn of the 20th Century to current discussions on sustainable development a century later. In chapter three we present some of the most important characteristics of today's environmental and natural resource problems. Here special attention is paid to modern society's mental and physical distancing from the natural environment. We tend to regard heating, water and food as are simply 'there' out of the wall when needed. Similarily, household waste etc. simply 'disappears' out of the wall. Nowadays, we mainly experience a physical connection with the natural environment in conjunction with such phenomena as 'outdoor recreation', 'outdoor education and 'nature-based tourism'.

1 The History of Humankind – from Hunting for Survival to Hunting for Pleasure

Do Humans Belong to the Animal Kingdom?

Are humans animals? Animals whose thin cultural façade constantly threatens to reveal the true being beneath the surface, especially in situations where we feel threatened, angry or sexually excited? Or is it possible that we have become sensible, cultured beings who have liberated ourselves from the restrictive bonds of nature? Free and rational beings who, with the help of science, systematically discover the mysteries of nature only to 'enhance' it with our technology and simply identify the resulting environmental situations and resource shortages as short term problems which will be solved 'some time in the near future'. Nils Uddenberg wrote the following response to the question of whether or not humans are animals:

> ...[that] humankind has inherited not only our bodies and to a great extent our uncontrollable 'animal urges' from our ape-like forefathers, but also our abilities to live together in society and to a degree, show some level of consideration towards each other.[1]

Most people, after giving the question a moment's thought, probably come to the conclusion that human beings are 'not just' animals. At the same time, however, they would have difficulty in claiming that human beings do not share any of their characteristics with animals. We eat, sleep and breathe in the same way as other animals – and it requires nothing more than a power cut to illustrate how dependent on and vulnerably exposed we are to our

---

1   Translated from Uddenberg (1998:9).

surroundings – our 'environment'. The way in which we see the relationship between humankind and nature – as well as the way in which we conduct that relationship – is of great importance, especially in matters of environmental and sustainable education. How do we actually see the natural world, humankind and the future? When evaluating such questions it is equally important to be aware of, for example, whether or not we see ourselves as animals, and how this affects our own values. A current issue which demonstrates this point is that of animal rights and the effects it has on questions related to the meat industry, humanism and human values.

This chapter will attempt to give a broad perspective of human history from the hunter-gatherer period up to the present day. It is a history during which humankind has, with the help of intellect and technology, established itself as an extremely (in the short term at least) successful species that inhabits almost all areas of the globe and, in comparison to other large mammals, in considerably large numbers. The chapter will conclude with a discussion on the principles of concepts such as 'nature', 'carrying capacity' and 'sustainability'.

Geological Time, Evolutionary Time, Human Time

We all know that time can pass both quickly and slowly, depending on the situation we find ourselves in. Five minutes at a fantastic party is completely different to five minutes waiting for a delayed train. Notwithstanding our ability to think in abstract terms, our own human form and similar frames of reference remain important to our understanding of the world. For example, a person who lives in a modern industrialised society can normally hope to reach about seventy or eighty years of age. Not reaching the age of twenty is a rarity, just as most people are not expected to live to much more than a hundred years old. These accepted facts have a great deal of influence on what we regard as 'a long time ago', 'the future' and 'in the long term'.

Three basic frames of references, relevant to both natural resources and the environment, are the geological, evolutionary and human time perspectives. The *geological time perspective* concerns the history of our planet, such as the formation of the continents, mountain chains etc. Even though this can seem to be a rather unimportant and forgotten period, we are still reminded of its characteristics and importance when volcanoes erupt or earthquakes take place. These forces of nature sometime manifest themselves in more modest ways, such as when revisiting a stretch of the Baltic Sea coast and noticing that the shoreline has been altered due to land elevation (a result of the great pressure exerted on the land during the Ice Age).

The evolutionary time perspective concerns the development of the species and their various adaptations to their respective environments. According to evolutionary theories, which we associate with Darwin,[2] there are always small hereditary differences between different individuals, and those individuals whose characteristics are more adapted to the environment in which they live can increase their chances of survival and reproduction. In this way these characteristics become increasingly dominant. Sometimes mutations can occur (genetic anomalies), which often lead to the chance of survival being reduced. However some of these transformations are successful and adapt themselves very well to their environments. It is these different forces which lie behind the reason for there being so many different species on the planet which have adapted to as many different conditions. This is a reason to support the claim that human beings share ancestry with the apes and that also today humans in many ways are animals. As with the geological perspective, the evolutionary perspective covers huge expanses of time during their stages of development.

The human time perspective is partly controlled by biology, e.g. the above example of a human life span, or that a generation is usually thought to be about 30 years (the time span during which children have grown up and had their own children). However, to a certain extent we are also controlled by the way in which different cultures regard time perspectives. The cultural aspects can include religious

2   Charles Darwin (1809–1882), British scientist and proponent of the theory of evolution.

influence and how we perceive the natural world. This affects how we prioritise the well-being of future generations and reflects decisions we make in the present. It addresses the way in which we put our trust into the development of future technologies – and whether we believe that future generations will be able to deal with and solve such problems as energy production or waste disposal that we today do not have sufficient understanding of.(There is also reason to believe that the 'short-term' perspective seems to receive more attention. in our modern industrial society, which is generally thought to have an ever-increasing pace of life – the word 'faster' has been suggested as a key word for understanding the 20th Century. The future plans of both authorities and businesses do not have to stretch too far into the future to be called 'long term' – a perspective that is almost impossible to relate to geological and evolutionary time frames!

The Hunter-gatherer Age

The longest period in the technological development of human beings is undisputedly the age of the hunter-gatherer. Perhaps we could date humankind's first act as a 'cultural being' back to 100,000 years ago – although even prior to this human beings had been using basic tools, weapons and fire for a long period. Yet there were still 60,000 years remaining before humans of the modern type of today moved into Europe, and some 90,000 years before the Ice Age was over in Northern Europe or the first agricultural societies were established in the Middle East.

Groups of people who live as hunters and gatherers must adapt to the landscape (the environment) and its characteristics, e.g. to the migrations of the animals which are hunted, the seasonal changes of both plants and weather and the availability of drinking-water and firewood. It is thought that in order to remain in one place for any length of time with sufficient provisions, yet equally be ready to move on when necessary and not to be too vulnerable; groups would have consisted of between perhaps 15 to 50 people. These groups would have made up a central tribe of hundreds or thousands of individuals that would have shared the same language and have gathered on certain occasions. The existence of this larger group would also have ensured a reduced risk of inbreeding.[3] The necessity of remaining mobile implied that there was neither time nor need to acquire many material belongings; status was often indicated in other ways than displaying a large collection of possessions.

The little we know of this type of technology, life style and world-view is, to a great extent, based on the information received from the remains of these cultural groups which still exist in our modern times on the fringes of the relentless spread of western 'civilisation' e.g. the indigenous populations of North and South America, Australia and Greenland. Partly due to today's environmental and natural resource issues, the approaches to the natural world shared by these groups has received a great deal of attention and become an important source of inspiration in promoting a more holistic view of nature and how we influence it.[4]

> The Wintu Indians said:...When we killed for meat, we ate everything. When we dug for roots, we made small holes. When we built houses, we dug shallow pits. We destroyed nothing, not even when we burnt grass to get grasshoppers. ... But white people tear up the earth, bring down trees: kill everything. The trees say: "Don't do it. I am suffering. Do not harm me" Yet they chop them down and cut them to pieces. The spirits of the land hate them.[5]

But it is also important not to romanticise the lives of these groups. Life was, beyond doubt, very hard from time to time, and even these primitive methods of utilising natural resources have led to species extinction and large-scale transformations in the landscape.[6]

> We left the polar bears in their kingdom of icebergs, and set off towards the winter hunting grounds ... You maybe think I had a small fish or a piece of musk-ox meat to eat? Don't make me laugh! I didn't

---

3   Inbreeding refers to the situation when biologically close related people have children – something which leads to the risk of hereditary diseases due to reduced genetic variation (compare with the above discussion about evolution).
4   See e.g. Millman (1987); and Chatwin (1998).
5   Translated from Persson (1973:26).
6   It is of course important to keep the long-term perspective in mind. For further reading see e.g. Grayson (2001) and Milberg & Tyrberg (1993). See also Worster (1994).

even have a strip to chew. The journey went on. It was hard work to drag the sledges along the lakes, around an island, over another island trudging on. ... This is our life, the hunter's life, travelling with the seasons.[7]

Humans in the Agricultural Age

The change from hunter-gatherer to farmer was, of course, a very long and continuously developing process. But also it brought with it a dramatic transformation of humankind's relationship towards the natural environment. People not only became permanent settlers, but they also 'invested' their time and energy into the land (digging ditches, building fences and houses, clearing stones from the fields etc.) – simultaneously there were now very strong reasons to defend territories and to acquire belongings and pass them on to the next generation. The philosopher Jean Jacques Rousseau wrote: 'The first person who fenced off a piece of land and called it his own gave rise to inequality among people and brought evil to the world.'[8]

A reccurring characteristic in the perception of nature among farming people was the aspect of fertility. The term 'Mother Earth' still provides us with a fully understandable analogy to demonstrate the relationship of close dependency that people had with the earth. With sun and rain, the earth produced everything that humans needed for their survival. The division between cultivated and uncultivated environments, with which we are now so accustomed to – tame and wild animals; plants and weeds; civilisation and wilderness etc. – is often linked with the interests of agricultural societies in distinguishing between friend and foe. It is worth pointing out how important this relationship of dependency with the natural world was extended to all areas of people's lives in this period. Too much or too little rain, predators attacking the livestock, early frosts etc., posed direct threats to the survival of a family or group. The ability to, or even an attempt to interpret the signs

---

7   Translated from Friberg (1982:53–54).
8   Jean Jacques Rousseau 1712–1778, translated quote from Sörlin (1992:20).

of nature was of great importance, as these interpretations determined both long and short term planning. The following verse is a direct translation (and therefore has no discernable rhyming pattern) taken from a Swedish book of farming (*Bondepraktikan*) from 1662:

> If you want to know how the winter will be
> On All Saints Day you must go to the forest
> And search for the beech tree
> And then you will see
> When you cut of a piece
> If it is dry, a warm winter is close
> But be the piece damp and wet
> There'll be a cold winter.

There was a large increase in population during the agricultural age, which led to the development of towns and cities and consequently changes in social and cultural aspects of life. There was also an increase in the number of professions and trades, which was of importance to the development of the various scientific and cultural innovations that had begun to appear e.g. writing, organised religions and educational establishments. New technological developments, as well as improved methods of communication over land and sea, led to the increase of supply and demand in both trade and information. However, permanent settlements with dense populations also allowed for the introduction and rapid spread of epidemics. Large-scale wars also appear, with devastating results. Famines could now easily effect entire populations as more and more people relied on the limited resources of farm produce as their main food source. These negative aspects of world history deserve attention as well as the positive sides.

The Growth of the Industrial Society

Industrialised society first began to emerge in Britain during the 18th Century. Other countries in western Europe did not become industrialised until the latter part of the 19th Century and the process is in many ways ongoing worldwide today. Compared with any other previous period in history this new approach to nature and landscape, characterised by the industrial age, is remarkably short.

If we look at the different methods of adaptation applied by humans to the environment in these three epochs, we see that the hunter-gatherers had to conform to demands of the environment and all its transformations; agricultural societies adapted to a certain extent to the environment, but they also transformed the land for their own needs; and industrialised society has, to the greatest extent, adapted the environment to fulfil human needs. One important characteristic of industrialised society is the various divisions of time for specific purposes (work, education, free time etc.) and divisions of space (workplace, schools, places for recreation etc.). Each of these specialised areas has been successively improved with a view to being more and more effective. All inputs for production, as well as goods and services (raw materials, know-how, fuel etc.), must be transported and coordinated and many of these procedures take place on a global scale.

Let's take, as an example, a modern industrial farm that has high wheat yields as its main priority. To achieve these ends the farm must use a great deal of energy and advanced technology. Everything which can interfere with the production must be reduced to a minimum: e.g. open drainage would be replaced with underground drainage systems, stones and unwanted bushes/trees would be removed, and weeds would be sprayed with chemicals. The result of this is an unprecedented level of efficiency. In order to have an idea of how much agricultural productivity has increased in modern industrial nations e.g. Sweden, we can observe that in the mid 18th Century the grain yields were approximately 700–800 kg per hectare, which would normally sustain 10–12 people. By the time of the introduction of industrialisation (late 19th Century) harvests had increased to approximately 1,500–2,000 kg per hectare, which would provide for between 20–25 people. A century later, in the late 20th Century, yields can be at least between 4,000–5,000 kg per hectare, which equals the calorific requirements of several hundred people.[9] This increase in productivity has especially characterised

9   Examples taken from the Swedish National Atlas, Agriculture (1992:7–9).

the last half of the 20th Century; e.g. milk production has more than doubled since the 1950's, as has the weight of farmed chickens.[10]

In industrialised agriculture, it is also possible to compensate for the various natural changes in the environment, which would have had devastating effects on pre-industrial farming, by using irrigation techniques and developing better seeds etc. However, there are now other areas of vulnerability e.g. a dependency on world oil and grain markets, changes in EU rulings on farm subsidies etc.

In the same way as the wheat field in the above example was organised for maximum efficiency, industrialised societies divide the landscape into specific designated areas for other specific functions, e.g. habitation (a housing estate or residential area), education (university facilities) and commerce (shopping centres). The countryside has also been adapted and developed for leisure activities (outdoor recreation, tourism etc.) that has become a central characteristic in modern society's relationship with nature, the environment and natural resources. All these specialised aspects are linked together with large, complex systems of transport, which in themselves require enormous amounts of fossil fuels and other resources if they are to function efficiently.[11]

In conclusion one may say that the level of vulnerability in a hunter-gatherer society was dictated by the availability of plants and animals. The level of vulnerability was reduced by these societies adopting a nomadic lifestyle and utilising a wide range of food sources. In order to maintain this lifestyle it was necessary to keep the population relatively low. In the pre-industrial agricultural societies, the level of vulnerability was controlled by keeping domestic animals (livestock), manipulating the ecosystem (cultivating the land) and storing supplies (e.g. earth cellars) as well as combining many ways of utilising local natural resources (hay making, chopping wood, fishing, hunting etc.). The level of vulnerability within a large city in an industrialised society, on the other hand, lies in the stability of its systems and methods of supply and main-

10 Swedish National Atlas, Agriculture (1992:74).
11 Fossil fuels e.g. oil (petrol, diesel etc.) cannot be reproduced within human time perspectives. This can be compared with renewable energy sources such as solar, wind and hydroelectric power.

tenance. It concerns a socio technical system of pipes, cables, administration, transportation, money, trust and contracts, which supplies the city and its inhabitants with water, heating, food, clothing, protection, building materials etc., and with a combination of air and water extraction systems, removes refuse, carbon dioxide, soot, toxins and sewage.

The Beginnings of the Post-industrial Age?

The extent that we, in our time, can reasonably discuss a new technological leap equal to that of the transition from the agricultural to the industrial society is a matter which has received a lot of attention during recent times. Is the industrial society now being replaced by a new 'post-industrial' society?[12]

Regardless of whether we see the changes taking place in today's society as aspects of a new and different society, or simply as changes which are a part of the process in the development of an industrial society, the fact remains that there are both negative and positive environmental issues at hand. The comparison between traditional letter writing (paper, envelopes, deliveries, airmail etc.) and the lightning speed of e-mails and other energy-efficient forms of communication serves as a good example of the potential we have of developing energy saving devices, which also require less raw materials in the production process. On the other hand, however, there is also an increasing level of vulnerability in the various systems/organisations within modern societies (multinational corporations, stock brokers, governments of the most powerful countries etc.) that are controlled by a shrinking number of very powerful people with increasing unpredictability. It is also important to realise that increased levels of production and consumption can rapidly cancel out any environmental improvements made in the processes of production and consumption. Reduced exhaust emis-

12 Post-industrial means literally 'after industrial', in the sense that it is a society which follows the industrial society. A 'post-modern' society indicates an even more radical change, whilst a term such as 'late-industrial' or 'late modern' merely refers to continued progress in the same conditions as characterised by the industrial society. See also chapter six and e.g. Lyon (1999).

sions as a result of technological advancements in the automobile industry will not lead to cleaner air if the number of cars on the road continues to rise. The possibility of watching television, downloading films and writing letters from the same computer does not necessarily imply that fewer screens will be used per household, as the likelihood of having a screen in every room is just as great. An increased level of awareness of environmental problems can result in a rise in demand for hotels and holiday destinations having 'environmentally friendly' certifications, but so can the number of tourists taking weekend holidays abroad exceed those who choose local destinations.[13] A central question, which arises here, is do we invest our increased technological potential in products or services, quantity or quality, fair or unfair distribution?

Where is Nature to be Found and What is an Environmental Problem?

Throughout the entire history of humankind, from the hunter-gathers to industrial society, the relationship towards what we today refer to as 'natural resources', 'the landscape' and 'the environment' has always been important. There have always been plenty of reasons for humans to observe and relate to the natural surroundings, even though these reasons and methods have changed considerably throughout the ages. – Will the deer return to this valley this year, and will we find fresh water before nightfall? Will the harvest be ready before the first frost, and will the sheep survive the wolves tonight? Is it acceptable to buy a second car with awareness of increasing greenhouse gases and the number of underprivileged people who lack any purchasing power at all, and how many toxins are there in the food products sold in the supermarket?

Environmental and natural resource problems have recurred as central themes in human history, and have always accompanied people and been important aspects of religion and philosophy. The main difference between our current age – the late-industrial period

13 See e.g. Frändberg (1998).

31

– and earlier epochs in history is the actual scale of environmental and natural resource issues. Non-renewable energy sources are continually exploited, raw materials and dangerous goods are transported across the globe and the effects of our methods of utilising the natural environment often have global consequences and will affect many future generations.

Current discussions on environmental and natural resource issues concern, to a great extent, how we relate to 'Nature'; this book itself addresses the need for bringing our attention to and encouraging the discussion of changes required in our approach to and use of nature. The fact that we regard 'society' and 'nature' as being two separate entities says a great deal about our perception of nature; such a viewpoint would probably be incomprehensible to the members of a traditional hunter-gatherer community.

It does not take much investigation into the various standpoints regarding the concept of 'nature' to see that they are grounded in cultural perceptions. In other words, what we actually mean when we say 'nature', whether we regard it as good or bad and whether it has intrinsic value or not, is given meaning and context within social 'negotiations' that take place between people.[14] Our perception of 'nature' depends on the society in which we live, how we were brought up, as well as the type of general knowledge and attitudes that we create (e.g. in schools). However, in that the actual concept of nature is culturally dependent, it does not imply that we are free to choose whether nature itself exists or not. People and society are dependent on their relationship with their environments, including those aspects which are beyond human control, e.g. everything from solar activity and the laws of gravity to the flight of migratory birds and the passage of streams down mountain sides.

The concept 'nature' is applied in a large number of contexts – many of which are quite contradictory. In any dictionary you can find a considerable list of its various definitions e.g. a state of nature,

14 One way of demonstrating how the concept of 'nature' is culturally constructed is to show how the understanding of what is nature and how our interaction with it should manifest itself, has varied over the years and between different groups, as well as how this has been incorporated into other dimensions of social debates. See e.g. Macnaghten & Urry (1998) and Grgas & Larsen (1994) for further reading on the subject.

being natural, the nature of things, the laws of nature etc. The following terminology will apply for the rest of this book (cf. fig 1:1).

- *Environment* = everything around us (incl. 'nature' and 'culture').
- *Nature* = the elements and processes in the environment that is not deliberately brought under human control (or, at least at present, could not be brought under human control). To some degree the concept of nature also includes landscapes that we interpret as mainly being characterised by such elements and processes, e.g. a rainforest (see further below).
- *Resources* = materials which are, given a certain society and technology, regarded as being of value to society and are extracted from the environment and transformed into the required state or form. If these materials come directly from nature (see the above definition) then these elements and processes become *natural resources*.
- *Environmental problems* = basically any problems with the surrounding environment which are encountered by people. However, to remain in keeping with common use of the term we reserve this concept to refer to environmental problems where it can be assumed that nature (see above definition) but also humans are directly involved in the situation. We regard 'natural catastrophes' such as earthquakes, tornadoes etc. as a separate category, as it is generally considered that humans have no influence on them.

Above we defined 'nature' as the elements and processes in the environment that people do not consciously control or govern.[15] This implies that nature is seen more as the elements and processes in any given environment and not as a specific area that can be demarcated in the landscape or on a map. Different environments comprise varying degrees of nature; from the relatively low levels e.g. inside a school and up to the higher levels e.g. in the Antarctic. We could see the move from the school to the Antarctic as a successive increase of natural elements, passing the environments of e.g. parks, forests and high mountains. It is noteworthy that even in an environment such as the inside of a school, 'nature' is present –

15   See Sandell (1988) for further details.

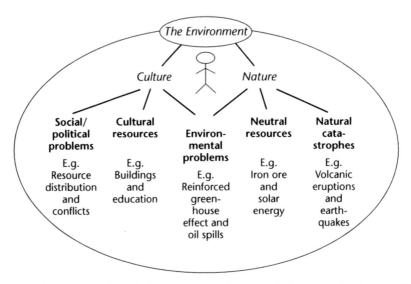

Figure 1:1 An overview of the contexts and usage of the terms 'environment', 'nature', and 'culture', as used in this book.

from the laws of gravity to a mouldy sandwich forgotten in someone's lunchbox, or, from the heartbeat of a teacher to the bugs in the changing-rooms. It is here important to be aware of the limited capacities of humans concerning control after all. One of the reasons for the above definition of nature is to accentuate the necessity of a conscious relationship with 'the uncontrolled'. Having said that, it is with a full understanding that both our bodies and our minds, and everything that is created from their interaction, originate from nature.

'The other' – culture, technology, society etc. – is correspondingly an expression for that which is directly created by humans. If we study the etymology of the terms, nature is associated with origins and birth, whilst culture is linked with cultivating (cf. 'culture' of bacteria). However, as the above definition of nature suggests, the boundaries between nature and culture (natural resources/cultural resources, natural landscapes/cultural landscapes, environmental/natural/cultural problems) are often unclear and varied. It is extremely difficult to determine the actual extent to which human

34

involvement has been one of the main causes of a transformation or a set of circumstances which we consider a problem, bearing in mind that for a great many years human activity (many times indirectly) has had an enormous impact on the environment (see chapter four).

From Muscle Power to Fossil Fuels to …

An important aspect of any environmental debate is 'energy'. A reminder of the entropy laws tells us that the energy actually could not be used but only transformed to a lower quality. So when discussing the use of energy we are actually focusing on the decreased quality of energy. Incoming solar energy is of very high quality, as opposed to the low quality energy of the heat that leaves our planet (see chapter four). But in line with common use of the term, we will here talk about the use of energy (meaning the quality of energy). If we look at the part that energy has played in human history, then the most important energy source for a very long time was *food*, which could be converted into muscle power (in order to hunt and in other ways gather more food) and *firewood*, which gave warmth, light and comfort. Successively other energy sources were utilised e.g. the *wind* that could power boats and mills, and *draught-animals* that only required feeding and in return could plough fields and transport heavy loads.

When the level of technology improved it meant that more people could be provided for within a specific region. For example, the introduction of agriculture or the transformation from a low resource agriculture to the use of, for example, irrigation that made it possible to support a larger population using the same area. However, in the face of these improvements the actual level of 'effectivity' was reduced in that more working hours (muscle power) were required to produce a certain quantity of food. Marshall Sahlins puts forward the idea of 'the original affluent society' where during the hunter-gatherer period it is believed that people could sustain themselves quite easily on just a few hours work a day.[16]

16 From Sörlin (1992:177 and 200) see also e.g. Boserup (1993) and Ellen (1982).

The great change in energy sources and usage, which came with the industrial revolution, was the replacement of renewable energy sources (plants and animals that were used for food, as well as firewood, wind and water). These were then to a large extent replaced with fossil fuels such as coal, and later on oil and nuclear power. It is apparent how much less dependent we are on physical labour in contemporary late-industrial society, e.g. in modern food production. We use our physical bodies so little in modern industrialised society today that it has instead become a great public health problem. The physical exertions of the early hunters and farmers (and draught-animals) have now been replaced with other energy sources. The actual energy balance – how much energy is expended in producing a fixed amount of food – has actually deteriorated in the industrial age.[17]

This chapter has illustrated how, with the help of technological development, the number of people which can be supported has steadily increased: from a population of around 10 million during the hunter-gatherer period to today's figure which is in excess of six billion. To use an ecological term, the *carrying capacity* has been raised (the number of a species, in this case human beings, which can be maintained within a certain area, see chapter four). The fact that humans have been able to raise the carrying capacity of the environment is, from an ecological point of view, unique. However, increased carrying capacity does not offer any information about the allocation of the world's resources; this topic will to some extent be addressed in the following chapter. There is also every reason to discuss how sustainable the present situation actually is, considering a steadily increasing global population in addition to an ever rising (and increasingly unequal) level of material consumption.

Further Reading

The wide ranges of scientific issues addressed in this chapter are studied in subjects such as human ecology and environmental history, and many of the sources used in the chapter are Swedish (e.g.

---

17 See e.g. Tivy & O'Hares' presentation (1981:89).

Sörlin, 1991 and 1992; Sandell & Sörlin, 2000: and Uddenberg, 1993 and 1998). General sources in English for further reading include e.g. Donald Worster's *The Wealth of Nature: Environmental History and the Ecological Imagination* (Oxford University Press, 1993) and Gerald Marten's *Human Ecology: Basic Concepts for Sustainable Development* (Earthscan, 2001) as well as Donald J Hughe's *An Environmental History of the World: Humankind's Changing Role in the Community of Life* (Routledge, 2001) and Ian Gordon Simmon's *Environmental History: A Concise Introduction* (Blackwell, 1993). With regard to the question of Man as nature or culture, further reading includes e.g.: *The Biophilia Hypothesis* (Kellert, S.R. & Wilson, E.O., Eds., Island Press/Shearwater Books, 1993), *Contested Natures* (Macnaghten, P. & Urry, J. Sage, 1998) or Steven Pinker's *The Blank Slate: The Modern Denial of Human Nature* (Penguin, 2002).

Another type of material which is receiving an increasing amount of interest, and that also touches upon human history, technological development and interaction between nature and culture, are certain types of computer games e.g. *Sofia's World* which takes a broad view of history of ideas as well as the various *SIM*-games, where one creates and runs entire cities, islands, national parks etc. There are also a number of historically based strategy games e.g. *Civilisation* and fantasy games such as *Myst, Riven* and *Arcanum* where one acts in mystical worlds using blends of old fashioned and future technologies. An important issue that must be raised (as these games probably have a lot of influence on children) is of course the manufacturers' outlook on humans, view of nature, environment and future development. These standpoints are always present, but are not always easy to identify and, therefore, relate to.

Other Reference Literature

Boserup, Ester (1993/1965). *The Conditions of Agricultural Growth: The Economics of Agrarian Change Under Population Pressure* (with a foreword by Robert Chambers). London: Earthscan Publications Ltd.

Chatwin, Bruce (1987). *The Songlines*. New York: Viking

Ellen, Roy (1982). *Environment, Subsistence and System: The Ecology of Small-Scale Formations*. Cambridge: Cambridge Univ. Press.

Friberg Gösta (1982). *Vi kommer att leva igen: Eskimå- och indian dikter från Berings hav till Panama: Urval och översättning av Gösta Friberg.* (We will live again: Eskimo and Indian poetry from the Bering Straits to Panama). Stockholm: FIB:s.

Frändberg, Lotta (1998). *Distance Matters: An inquiry into the relation between transport and environmental sustainability in tourism.* Humanekologiska skrifter No. 15. Göteborg, Sweden: Göteborg University.

Grayson, Donald K. (2001) The Archaeological Records of Human Impacts on Animal Populations. *J. of World Prehistory,* Vol. 15, No. 1, pp. 1–68.

Grgas, Stipe & Larsen, Svend Erik (eds.) (1994). *The Construction of Nature: A Discursive Strategy in Modern European Thought.* Odense, Denmark: Odense University press.

Lyon, David (1999). *Postmodernity.* Minneapolis: University of Minnesota Press.

Macnaghten, Phil & Urry, John (1998). *Contested Natures.* London: Sage.

Milberg, Per & Tyrberg, Tommy (1993). Naïve birds and noble savages: A review of man-caused prehistoric extinctions of island birds. *Ecography* Vol. 16, No. 3, pp. 229–250.

Millman, Lawrence (1987). *A Kayak Full of Ghosts: Eskimo Tales Gathered and Retold by Lawrence Millman.* Santa Barbara: Capra Press.

Persson, Lars (1973). *Lyssna, Vite Man!* (Listen, White Man!). Stockholm: Pan/Nordstedts.

Sandell, Klas (1988). *Ecostrategies in Theory and Practice: Farmers' Perspectives on Water, Nutrients and Sustainability in Low-resource Agriculture in the Dry Zone of Sri Lanka.* Linköping, Sweden: Linköping Studies in Arts and Science, No. 19.

Sandell, Klas & Sörlin, Sverker (Eds.) (2000). *Friluftshistoria – fråm'härdande friluftsliv' till ekoturism och miljöpedagogik: Teman i det svenska friluftslivets historia.* (The history of outdoor recreation – from 'the tough outdoor life' to eco tourism and environmental pedagogic: Themes in Swedish outdoor history). Stockholm: Carlssons.

The National Atlas of Sweden: *Agriculture* (1992). Stockholm: National Atlas of Sweden Publishing.

Sörlin, Sverker (1991). *Naturkontraktet: Om naturumgängets idéhistoria.* (The contract with nature: on the history of humans' relationship with nature). Stockholm: Carlssons.

Sörlin, Sverker (Ed.) (1992). *Humanekologi: Naturens resurser – människans försörjning.* (Human ecology: Nature's resources – humans' maintenance). Stockholm: Carlssons.

Tivy, Joy & O'Hare, Greg (1981). *Human Impact on the Ecosystem.* Edinburgh: Oliver & Boyd.

Uddenberg, Nils (1993). *Ett djur bland andra? Biologin och människans uppfattning om sin plats i naturen.* (An animal among others? Biology and the humans' understanding of their place in nature). Nora, Sweden: Nya Doxa.

Uddenberg, Nils (1998). *Arvsdygden: Biologisk utveckling och mänsklig gemenskap.*(Biological development and human community). Stockholm: Natur och Kultur.

Worster, Donald (1994). *Nature's Economy: A History of Ecological Ideas.* Cambridge: Cambridge University Press.

2 The History of Industrialism and Environmentalism

Control Through Understanding

Towards the end of the last chapter, we stated that humans, with the help of technology, have the extraordinary ability to raise the carrying capacity (the ability to support more people or consume more per capita). Humans can literally 'make bread from stones', e.g. by using coal (*stones*) as an energy source for an industry which produces tractors that can be used together with a number of other items (refined seeds, pesticides, fertilizer etc.) to produce large amounts of wheat, which can in turn be used to bake *bread*.

Industrial development requires a combination of craftsmanship and scientific knowledge. An important factor in this has been a perception of the natural world and an idea of development, which is in agreement with a mechanical and progressive-optimistic worldview. The mechanistic approach to the world (or mechanistic view of nature) is understood in terms of nature being a large complicated machine and the environment as being an intricate – but principally understandable – mechanism of which different parts can 'break down', 'be exchanged' or 'be repaired' by humans and at the discretion of humans. It is both interesting and important to introduce a gender perspective here, as it is clear that this exploitative, scientific and mechanical worldview has a great deal in common with the male patriarchal perspective.[1]

The idea of ongoing human advancement and the perspective that humans can continually develop and improve society is often dated back to the scientific discoveries in the 17th Century and the Enlightenment in the 18th Century. Nowadays, the idea that society

---

1   See e.g. Merchant (1980).

and technology will continue to develop positively is so deeply entrenched in the industrial society that the only reason one needs to buy a product is simply because it is 'new' (new computer software, new type of running shoes etc.), when the only thing we can be completely sure of is that when something is new it is relatively untested.

Issues of environmental ethics, perceptions of nature and development will be addressed in the next section of the book (Part II), although we can underline the enormous influence of the Enlightenment on modern society's relationship to nature, with its focus on reason and factual investigations/experimentations (empiricism). We can e.g. remind ourselves of the actual purpose of the renowned scientist Carl Linnaeus's travels through Sweden during the 18th Century, which was to make an inventory of the country's resources in an attempt to replace foreign imports with domestic production.[2] We can also refer to the words of the 17th Century English philosopher, Francis Bacon, who said that by means of science, humankind should learn to control and command nature by obeying her.[3] To some degree, this perspective can be said to predict the tendency of humans to follow the short term approach and exploit the world's natural resources with the help of science and advanced technology. However Bacon's statement is also reflected in today's systematic and scientific understanding of the mechanics of the natural world and the relationship of dependency which humans have with nature, in terms of systems ecology, environmental research and environmental protection (even though, in all probability, it wasn't what Bacon actually meant).

What the expression of controlling nature does not imply, however, is a more critical approach to technology and economic growth that has been an underlying feature of the growth of environmental movements. Even though objections against emotionless science and blind materialism have been present throughout the entire development of the industrial society (e.g. the Swiss-French philosopher Jean-Jacques Rousseau's criticism of civilisation and his 'back to nature'-message), it was only when industrialism really began to transform the landscape, through urbanisation,

2   Carl Linnaeus, 1707–1778.
3   Taken from Frängmyr (1980:42).

huge polluting factories and the building of railways, that environmental debate in recently established industrial nations became serious.

The remainder of this chapter will focus on this growth of the human commitment of protecting and preserving the environment that has developed along with the establishment of industrialised nations. An historical perspective is always beneficial and this is proven here, as we will see in the historical ideas that still prevail and are also intrinsic elements in current environmental debates. The actual extent to which a product or activity can be regarded as 'environmentally friendly' is decided by how the term is defined – the depth and detail which is demanded in each environmental standpoint. Deciding whether or not something is environmentally friendly, such as driving a car with a catalytic converter, depends on comparisons with, for example, cars without catalytic converters. But we can also compare using ethanol in cars instead of fossil fuels or using hydroelectricity to power trains for transports. The same applies to sorting household refuse for recycling compared with throwing everything away together, or adapting one's lifestyle in order to drastically reduce the amount of waste which is produced.

Nature Preservation and National Landscapes

The latter years of the 19th Century saw the introduction of the perspective of nature preservation in western Europe and North America. In the USA the Yellowstone National Park was established as early as 1872 and in Sweden the nature preservation act and national parks were introduced in 1909. Links between nature preservation and members of society's elite were common. It was considered important to create a national identity and to experience landscapes characterised by nature. Outdoor recreation and tourism were important elements in achieving this. In North America, there was an interest in being able to preserve the experience of 'the frontier' for future generations– the pioneers' close contact and struggle with 'the wilderness' was therefore one of the main reasons for establishing national parks. This was clearly a perspective that totally ignored the indigenous populations and their relationship with the land.

Here it is important to see the strong ties to the development of the tourist industry e.g. the Norwegian tourist association was established as early as 1868 and prior to that the British upper classes had been journeying to the Swiss Alps and the mountains of Norway to hunt and fish. The reasons for these new activities were partly due to the ability of the upper classes to access the countryside by trains and steamboats, but there was also the establishment of a new way of relating to countryside, the urge to seek out 'the primitive' and 'to be close to nature'. This new approach was partly inspired by the romantics' interest in natural states and the wilderness and was what we today associate with outdoor life and nature-based tourism.

In short, we see the establishment of a perspective on nature and the countryside where certain areas (e.g. national parks), locations and objects (natural monuments), and species (e.g. protected species) are *protected* from the large scale and increasingly dramatic transformations that are undeniable features of the Industrial Age. In addition, there was also the criticism of modernisation itself (urbanisation, industrialisation, internationalisation etc.). Those people who advocate the latter perspective would prefer to focus on the traditional local and rural perspectives and had a great respect for pre-industrial society, handicrafts, small scale farming etc. However, with the help of inventories, collections, reserves and exhibitions, most of the interest in this direction was towards opening museums. The opening of 'Skansen', the Swedish open-air museum in Stockholm in 1891, which was the first of its kind in the world and displays the variations in culture, geography, flora and fauna of Sweden, together with animal protection programmes and reserves in the countryside, can be seen as good examples of the commitment to nature preservation.[4]

Another important item on the agendas of early industrialism's equivalent of today's environmentalism included the increasing health and hygiene problems in the rapidly expanding cities of the

---

4   The information on 'Skansen' is taken from Rantatalo & Åkerberg (2002); see also Åkerberg (2001).

time. Initially sewerage and refuse processing was dealt with much in the same way as people were accustomed to in the countryside. As the buildings became higher and higher the rows of outdoor toilets (privies) became longer and longer. With the passage of time it became clear that some kind of organised method of waste disposal was necessary, and the water closet, which was introduced around 1900, became an important symbol of this new approach.

Nature Conservation and Recreation

Parallel with the successive democratisation of modern industrial society, the extension of the right to vote (suffrage) also led to an increase in the general public's interaction with natural environments in their free time. In Sweden, for example, an important holiday act was introduced in the 1930s and there was more attention given to the countryside surrounding urban areas and women and children were encouraged to participate. The earlier, more adventurous and scientific approach to outdoor recreation, gave way to a more 'social' attitude. The fact that the majority of the population now had moved into cities in order to work in the industries there, and workers' movements were calling for vacations and holidays, were important determining factors in these changes. Carl Fries wrote the following in 1935, about the shift from upper class interest in nature to larger, more diverse groups in society being able to experience this type of first hand contact with the natural environment.

> For those who remember the idyllic years before the war [before the First World War] when the summer guests resembled beings from another world. ...[They arrived] in the midst of the simple rural life with huge amounts of luggage, strange behaviour and fine, new clothes. They took walks in the meadows, bathed in the lakes and fished in the midday sun in places where fish never took the bait. ... Now all is different. From every town and community, Saturday, Sunday week after week, hundreds even thousands make for the countryside, the forests, lakes and meadows."[5]

5 Carl Fries from the Swedish anthology *Vi och vår natur* (We and our nature; 1935:206).

Simultaneously, engagement in conservation shifted towards regarding humans as being more active participants in the formation of the countryside. Now there was less attention on collecting and protecting specific objects and locations for nature preservation. This had given way to an approach more oriented towards deciding which values should be adhered to – especially since some of these values in the landscape obviously were closely linked to human activities and rural culture e.g. pastures and meadows. It was not enough, then, to conserve and protect certain natural interests. They also had to be cared for otherwise the natural process of time would erode the values (e.g. a meadow will become overgrown without cultivation).

Environmental Protection and Peak Years

After the Second World War, there was an extremely rapid increase in material growth in the industrialised countries. The years leading up to 1973 (the year OPEC introduced a drastic increase in oil prices) are sometimes referred to as 'the peak years', and it is argued that never before had so many people experienced such an increase in material standards in such a short time. Car ownership became common and has since been a classic symbol of economic status – and in later years also a symbol of environmental damage. Littering, not least alongside roads, also became an important parallel issue.

Regarding the issues of nature and the environment, it became more apparent that measures could not be isolated to certain places, areas or species. It is of little use if birds of prey and their habitats are protected, if they cannot produce offspring due to their prey being poisoned by seeds in fields which have been treated with mercury based pesticides. There was now also a growing interest in what is called systems ecology (see chapter four). Even if ecology, as a branch of science, dates back to the mid 19th Century,[6] systems

---

6   Ecology: the branch of biology dealing with the relations of organisms to one another and to their environment; Ernst Haeckel (1834–1919) is said to have coined the term in 1866.

ecology introduced new theories and models that were now widely applicable. Since then, terminology such as 'food chain' and 'eco-system' are important elements in environmental debates and environmental teaching. In this spirit of systems ecology and other comprehensive approaches towards the environment, the 1960s saw the establishment of governmental institutions as well as legislation with the aim of conservation and the increased awareness of environmental issues. At around this time in Sweden there was e.g. the introduction of what is known as 'the National Land-use Planning' which, in 1972, lead to an all encompassing plan of action as regards what interests were to be prioritised in various parts of the country (e.g. on which stretch of coast there were to be industrial developments and which stretches were to be allocated for recreational purposes). It can be added here that in Sweden, from this point onwards, all future planning was to be based on 'what appears to be the correct decision from an *ecological* point of view'.[7]

Critical Alternatives

Despite the apparent interest, shown in the above, for choosing a perspective based on systems ecology the debates in nature and environment conservation had, until the 1970s, been mainly concerned with 'symptoms'. There was increasing consensus in the fact that the negative side effects of industrialism could be serious – hydroelectric dams, toxic emissions into air and water, poisons in the food chains, de-forestation etc. There were various attempts to tackle these side effects through legislation, research, restrictions, and monitoring of industrial activity by the authorities. However the actual development, the modern prioritisation of material and economic growth, urbanisation and industrialisation was seldom questioned.

Of course a few lone critical opponents were heard, from 19th Century criticisms of civilisation to the early alarm bells of the

---

7   Official government report 1971 no. 75, p. 27 [emphasis in original].

1950s and 60s,[8] although it was not until the 1970s that modern criticisms towards the actual question of development were brought up more generally. Some of this criticism stemmed from a widespread, internationally oriented radicalisation [9] (e.g. the student revolt in France in 1968 and the protests in a number of countries against the US military operations in Vietnam). Generally there was a sharp increase in the amount of new environmental and other activist movements.

In 1971, *Fältbiologerna* – the Nature and Youth Sweden, launched a campaign against the unchecked wastage of resources. This did not just address the symptoms of industry, it concerned all aspects of nature and the environment and even, to a great extent, the general development of society, which at this point was fully adapted to disposable products, material gain and non-stop consumerism. Additionally, as a result of the above, there was the growing problem of increased dependence on fossil fuels (oil), the amount of waste being produced and the danger of toxins being released into the atmosphere and river systems etc. The new radical environmental groups began to demand 'alternatives' which initially represented a negation of the present conventional development strategy. 'Green groups' countered urbanisation by moving into the country, agribusiness was countered with alternative farming without the use of chemical fertilizers etc. and wind farms and hydro electricity were presented as valid alternative energy sources instead of non-renewable (oil, coal and nuclear power). There were also many other alternative engagements e.g. in housing, trade, city planning etc. It was seen as important that the chosen alternative goals would encompass international solidarity, responsibility for future generations, quality of life and non-material values and oppose the prevailing attitude of short term material consumption. There was also the link with peace conflicts, issues which can never be ignored, as all forms of war and oppression are in complete con-

8   Ex. Carson (1962) and in Sweden e.g. Wägner (1941); Borgström (1953) and Palmstierna (1967). These authors were very critical to the effects of modern civilisation and displayed links between resource issues, perspectives on development and lifestyles. Particularly noteworthy is Elin Wägner's early presentation of the connections between the gender perspective, environmentalism and pacifism.

9   L Radix = root; to get to the root of the matter.

trast to what has later come to be known as sustainable development.

We can see these alternative currents as an example of what the peace and development researcher, Björn Hettne, has termed a 'counter point'; a critical voice against the mainstream development of society.[10] One of the projects at this time was called '*Alternativt Norden*' (Nordic Alternative), which attempted to develop interest in reconstructing the whole development strategy of society in favour of more locally based self-reliance strategies (this included criticism of the EC, the forerunner of the EU) to be carried out in direct contact with similar organisations in third world countries. The nuclear power debate became a very hot topic which exposed a great deal of criticism from those who were opposed to a future nuclear powered society with all the aspects of environmental damage, security problems and the passing of nuclear waste on to future generations.[11]

1972 became an important year, as the United Nations Conference on the Environment took place in Stockholm. People began to take the links between environmental and developmental issues more seriously; something that became an established fact with the follow up conference in Rio de Janeiro in 1992 (see the heading 'sustainable development'). In the same year, 1972, the environmental group Greenpeace was formed, the report of the Club of Rome 'The Limits to Growth' was published, the world's oldest environmental political party was established in New Zealand[12] and in Norway, Erik Damman's book, 'The Future in our Hands', was published – and which also gave its name to the movement which has since spread to a number of other countries.[13] It can be said that since 1972, environmental issues have been globalised, and the grassroots movements' slogan, 'think globally act locally', is still relevant, at least as an ideal in most of the current discussions on natural resources and the environment.

---

10   Hettne (1982). See also Hettne (1994) for an overview of the different perspectives of development incl. the characteristics of the alternative viewpoints.
11   An important event which underlined this debate was the nuclear reactor accident at Harrisburg (Three Mile Island), USA, in 1979.
12   The Green Party of Aotearoa, under the name of The Values Party.
13   The book was republished in 1978 and published in English the following year (Damman, 1979)

Sustainable Development

Since the UN conference in Rio in 1992, 'sustainable development' has been a central concept in all matters concerning the environment and natural resources. As an important reference point, the work carried out by the Brundtland Commission is usually referred to (the Norwegian Prime Minister Gro Harlem Brundtland was the chairman of the commission). They presented their final report, *Our Common Future*, in 1987. It was in this report that the now ubiquitous definition of sustainable development was first introduced

> Sustainable development is development that meets the needs of the present without compromising the ability of future generations to meet their own needs. It contains two key concepts:
>
> – the concept of 'needs', in particular the essential needs of the world's poor, to which overriding priority should be given; and
> – the idea of limitations imposed by the state of technology and social organisation on the environment's ability to meet present[14]

How radical is the concept of sustainable development if we compare it with the aforementioned perspectives (nature preservation, nature conservation, environmental protection and critical alternatives)? It is quite clearly more comprehensive than perspectives of preservation and conservation. However, if we look at the perspectives of environmental protection and the critical alternatives, it is more difficult to judge. On the one hand it can be said that the idea of sustainable development has a clear international dimension and this implies that it extends further than the more national perspectives of environmental protection. Whereas on the other hand, there is little doubt that many participants who are involved in the current discussions of the necessity of sustainable development do not adopt or accept many of the alternative demands for a radical review of the objectives and means of industrialised societies of today.

A good illustration of the friction within the concept of sustainable development – between a globalised version of treating the symptoms of industrialised societies (in line with environmental protection) and the alternatives held by environmentalists, which

14   World Commission on Environment and Development (1987: chapter two).

demand fundamental changes in the priorities of industrialised societies – is supplied by the Norwegian philosopher, Arne Naess, in his differentiation between 'shallow' and 'deep' ecology. He describes the shallow and less radical ecology as being engaged in projects such as combating pollution and a more efficient and equal distribution of resources, in addition to stabilising the global population. He also points out that advocates of this approach tend to offer narrow technical and scientific explanations, which are supposed to serve as solutions to problems. According to Naess, in addition to the requirements of the shallow movement, the deep ecological movement also represents a large number of much more radical perspectives, such as a classless society, autonomy, decentralisation, self-support, protection of all cultures, respect for life etc.[15]

Naess refers to his perspective as *ecosophy*,[16] and the ties between ecology and philosophy are quite clear in this perspective. With reference to what was said above about 1972 being a key year for environmentalism, we can even note the fact that "Ecosophy was introduced by Arne Naess in 1972 during an ecophilosophy talk at a conference...".[17] A way of describing sustainable development's current position and content is to see it as an ongoing struggle between different versions of these two perspectives (the shallow vs. the deep ecology). The actual struggle (discussions, debates, conflicts) can also be seen as parallels of the terms 'mainstream' and 'counterpoint', which appeared earlier in the text. In other words it is a question of how radical the changes must be in order for them to be considered as sustainable. On one side we have powerful groups such as multinational corporations, governments and various influential pressure groups and think tanks who feel that it is sufficient to suggest and/or follow relatively superficial guidelines concerning changes in attitudes or distribution of power. In contrast, those with opposing opinions feel that it is necessary to introduce comprehensive changes in areas such as consumption, lifestyles and international relationships. Examples of the more radical 'alternative' perspectives which are, to a relatively small extent, vis-

15 Naess (1973) and (1989).
16 Actually 'ecosophy-T', in order to emphasise that there could be more than one ecosophy and that this is a point based on the idea of the importance of diversity. See also e.g. Reed & Rothenburg (1993).
17 Drengson (1997:110).

ible in our daily lives, include the selections of environmentally friendly, "organic", and other similar labelled products on sale, or the possibility of being able to choose environmentally friendly electricity from e.g. wind farms.

It was mentioned in the above that the early 'alarm bells' concerning a modern, global and development oriented commitment to natural resources and environmental issues emerged in the 1950s and 60s, and that they were the precursors of the new environmental movements which appeared in the 1970s. Following that, mainly during the 1980s, these issues began to be absorbed by mainstream political parties and they appeared in surveys and on news programmes. The general public seemed to have, at least verbally, developed a sense of commitment to the environment. Nowadays, we have a situation where one can say, without exaggeration, that there are almost no politicians, company executives, or teachers who, whilst maintaining political correctness, can claim to have no interest at all in current environmental issues. Even though it might be a case of just paying lip service to sustainable development, it is still an omnipresent element in the global community. To summarise, we have a situation where the current recognition of the necessity of sustainable development can be said to consist of elements and tensions between all the main themes which have been mentioned as being representative of the growing commitment to the environment (fig. 2:1).

Reserves and Multipurpose Use

In accordance with the perspectives subscribed by sustainable development, environmental issues are a permanent feature in the whole of society's discussion on development and management. Sustainable development should therefore be just as much an integral part of e.g. the national economy, sociology, history, legislation, philosophy, social science and business economics as it is a part of biology, ecology and geography. What, then, has become of the 'old' perspectives of nature preservation and conservation with reserves, protection schemes and socially beneficial aspects of contact with nature (outdoor recreation and public health etc.)? We

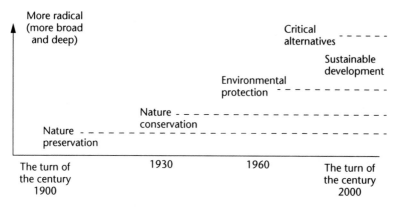

Fig. 2:1 Main themes in the development of modern environmental commitment. Even though these perspectives can, in the main, be associated to specific time periods, some sources of inspiration go far back in time, and, as shown in the illustration, have an influence on later periods. In short, they are all constituents in the current debates about nature, the environment and sustainable development.

should first state that issues such as preservation and conservation schemes, as well as recreational activities, are still very important; they are objects of political engagement, they receive attention in social planning and are essential elements in increasing the quality of many people's lives. However, we should also state that the traditional distinguishing features between nature and non-nature (e.g. between nature conservation and the conservation of a cultural monument) are becoming increasingly difficult to separate. The introduction of systems ecology has had quite an impact on this, to the extent that it is no longer possible to whittle the discussion of nature conservation down to the mere establishment of a nature reserve. Together with the fact that, during the 20th Century, democratisation has received more recognition, we can see that traditional reserves, such as. National Parks are nowadays not always as readily accepted by local populations. On the contrary, they could be seen to represent the dubious interests of outsiders who aim to cheat local populations out of their native lands.[18]

18   For a Swedish case study see e.g. Sandell (2001).

53

Alongside this development, however, an increasing assortment of protection programmes and types of reserves are associated with various international organisations, such as UNESCO's biosphere reserves and world heritage projects, or the EU's Natura 2000-areas. As in the case of the biosphere programmes, it is not just a case of protecting and conserving the natural environment, but is more a case of evaluating which demands are placed on a certain region by the introduction of sustainable development, and then based on that information determine which areas of the landscape should definitely not be exploited.[19] These types of project can be seen as approaching a level of diversity, where natural and cultural interests and the needs of protection and development/utilisation are working together in the same area. All this remains in complete contrast to the basic characteristic of industrialism, which increasingly divides the landscape into specific areas for specific production purposes, e.g. adventure tourism, iron ore extraction and grain production, often designated on a global scale.

Globalisation

In this chapter we have followed the development of modern commitment towards conserving and protecting the environment and its successive expansion and advancement. It must be said that it is difficult to make any predictions and/or definitions of current and future environmental projects, although here we will try to highlight some of the relevant characteristics of the current situation. The global perspective that we identified as being a salient characteristic during the radicalisation periods of the 1970s is a major topic in current discussions. At that time, however, the alternative environmentalists also included aspects of local independence and self-support in their debate to a much larger extent than is done today. An important future issue will doubtless be how the relationship between local activities (housing, foodstuffs, planning etc.) and the more large-scale aspects of a global sustainable development will manifest itself, or quite simply, what about the 'geo-

19 See e.g. Price (1996).

graphical' or 'spatial' perspectives on future sustainable development? What we today refer to as 'globalisation' can by and large be seen as a continuation of what we discussed earlier as fundamental characteristics of industrialism in terms of functional specialisation and a large- scale exchange of resources and products.

An important aspect of the current discussions on globalisation – a discussion which is to a great extent a question of 'sustainable development' and its content – lies in the differences between those who hold critical views of globalisation and those who are simply negative towards it. To quote the peace researchers and debaters, Hans Abrahamson and America Vera-Zavalas:

> The important point regarding Seattle [the demonstrations during the World Trade Organisation meeting] was that the event showed the mutual interests between, on the one hand, the groups who have a negative opinion of globalisation and, on the other hand, those who support the need for a different kind of globalisation.[20]

Among the groups here referred to as being negative towards globalisation are those trade unions who "have profited from the unfair exchange in international trade, especially as long as the demands made on clients regarding free trade and deregulation did not apply to them".[21] This is in contrast to those who hold critical views on globalisation and "are working towards real globalisation, fairness and equality".[22] This tension between, so to speak, an egotistical and a common cause approach of the criticism to globalisation, will most likely have a large part in the continued discussions concerning the direction of future global development. Quite often there are clear links between the 'common cause' criticisms of globalisation and the perspectives of what was referred to earlier as the 'alternative' and 'deep ecology' movements.[23]

Another aspect of the current globalisation discussion – of particular relevance from an educational perspective – is the importance of not having a limited scope of what is considered to be an 'engagement'. The international network organisations of youth movements that hold critical views of globalisation are good exam-

---

20 Translated from Abrahamson & Vera- Zavala (2001:34).
21 Ibid.
22 Ibid.
23 See e.g. Klein (2000).

ples of how one can be actively involved without necessarily having to be a member of more conventional organisations or, indeed, political parties.

Further Reading

Examples of literature which address the development of environmental commitment, the history of ideas and the links between science, industrial societies, environmental issues and views of nature include: *The Roots of Modern Environmentalism* by David Pepper (Routledge, 1993) and *The Wealth of Nature: Environmental History and the Ecological Imagination* by Donald Worster (Oxford University Press, 1993). Also of interest might be e.g. *The Making of a New Environmental Consciousness: A Comparative Study of the Environmental Movements in Sweden, Denmark and the Netherlands* (Jamison, A.; Eyerman, R. & Cramer, J., Edinburgh University Press, 1990), *The Making of Green Knowledge, Environmental Politics and Cultural Transformation* (Jamison, A., Cambridge University Press, 2001) and *Changing Environmental Behaviour* (Lundgren, L.J. Ed., Swedish Environmental Protection Agency and others, 1999). For outdoor recreation, national parks, wilderness and nature tourism, especially in North America see e.g. *Back to Nature: The Arcadian Myth in Urban America* (Schmitt, P.J., Oxford University Press, 1969) and *Wilderness and the American Mind* (Nash, R., Yale University Press, 1982). With regard to Sweden see *Friluftshistoria – från härdande friluftslif till ekoturism och miljöpedagogik: Teman i det svenska friluftslivets historia* (The history of outdoor recreation – from 'the tough outdoor life' to eco tourism and environmental pedagogy: Themes in Swedish outdoor history; Sandell, K. & Sörlin, S. (Eds.) Carlssons, 2000).

Other Reference Literature

Abrahamason, Hans & Vera-Zavala, America (2001). Demoniseringen av solidaritet (The demonisation of solidarity). *Le Monde Diplomatiques* svenska utgåva, No. 8, s. 32–34.

Borgström, Georg (1953). *Jorden – vårt öde* (The earth – our destiny). Stockholm: Forum.

Carson, Rachel (1962). *Silent Spring*. Boston.

Damman, Erik (1979). *The Future in Our Hands.* Oxford: Pergamon Press (Original: Fremtiden i våre hender, 1972).

Drengson, Allan (1997). An Ecophilosophy Approach, the Deep Ecology Movement and Diverse Ecosophies. *The Trumpeter*, Vol. 14, No. 3, pp. 110–111.

Frängsmyr, Tore (1980). *Framsteg eller förfall, framtidsbilder och utopier I västerländsk tanketradition* (Progress or decline, future images and utopias in western traditions of thought). Stockholm: Liber.

Hettne, Björn (1982). *Strömfåra och kontrapunkt i västerländsk utvecklingsdebatt.* (Mainstream and counter point in western development debate). Stockholm: Naturresurs- och miljökommitténs bakgrunds rapport, No.8.

Hettne, Björn (1994). The Future of Development Studies. *Forum for Development Studies*, No. 1–2, pp. 41–41.

Klein, Naomi (2000). *No Logo: No space, no choice, no jobs, taking aim at the brand bullies.* London: Flamingo.

The Limits to Growth: A Report for the Club of Rome's Project on the Predicament of Mankind. (1972). New York: The Club of Rome.

Merchant, Carolyn (1980). *The Death of Nature: Women, ecology, and the scientific revolution.* San Francisco: Harper & Row.

Naess, Arne (1973). The Shallow and the Deep, Long-Range Ecology Movement: A Summary. *Inquiry*, Vol. 16, pp. 95–100.

Naess, Arne (1989). *Ecology, community and lifestyle: Outline of an ecosophy* (translated and revised by David Rothenburg). Cambridge University Press, Cambridge (Original: Økologi og filosofi, Oslo, 1973).

Palmstierna, Hans (1967). *Plundring, svält, förgiftning* (Plunder, starvation, poisoning). Stockholm: Rabén & Sjögren.

Price, Martin F. (1996). People in Biosphere reserves: An evolving concept. *–Society and Natural Resources*, Vol. 9, pp. 645–654.

Rantatalo, Petra & Åkerberg, Sofia (2002). "Ansikte mot ansikte med de verkliga tingen" – Folkskolans åskådningsundervisning, Skansen och den nya nationalismen ("Face to face with the real things" – the teaching by object-lessons in the elementary school, Skansen and the new nationalism). *Lychnos*: Årsbok 2001 för idé- och lärdoms historia, p. 7–40.

Reed, Peter & Rothenburg, David (Eds.) (1993). *Wisdom in the Open Air: The Norwegian Roots of Deep Ecology.* Minneapolis, London: University of Minnesota Press.

Sandell, Klas (2001). The Non-establishment of a Kiruna National Park 1986–89: A Discussion of Tourism, the Right of Public Access and Regional Development. Paper presented at the Kiruna session of *the Travel & Tourism Research Association (TTRA) Conference* "Creating and Managing Growth in Travel & Tourism" April 22–25, 2001, Sweden.

SOU (Statens Offentliga Utredningar) (Official Government Reports). (1971) No. 75. *Hushållning med mark och vatten* (Economizing with land and water). Stockholm: Civildepartmentet.

Vi och vår natur (1935). (We and our nature). Stockholm: Bonniers.

Wägner, Elin (1941). *Väckarklocka* (Alarm Clock). Stockholm: Bonniers.

World Commission on Environment and Development (1987). *Our Common Future*. Oxford: Oxford University Press.

Åkerberg, Sofia (2001). *Knowledge and Pleasure at Regent's Park: the Gardens of the Zoological Society of London During the Nineteenth Century*. Idéhistoriska skrifter No. 36, Umeå, Sweden: Umeå Universitet.

3 Sustainable Development – Sustainable for Who?

Social, Economical and Ecological Sustainability

In the previous chapter, it was made clear that the concept of 'sustainable development' covers an extensive range of issues; it can not be restricted to 'nature' topics such as nature reserves, preservation or littering, and neither is it adequate to limit the concept to e.g. national legislation and sewage treatment works. It was also stated that one way of becoming better acquainted with both the content and the current debate on these environmental perspectives is to examine the relationship between what was referred to as 'deep' and 'shallow' ecology, respectively.[1] Also, it was added that even if one does not fully accept the deep ecology's radical stipulations for new priorities to be adopted within society, it is still necessary to regard sustainable development as a comprehensive concept. A common practice is to at least acknowledge an *economical*, a *social* and an *ecological* dimension of sustainable development. The concept must, then, concern the question of distribution – e.g. between rich and poor and generations – or politics in the broader sense of the term. Based on the standpoint that people want to pay more attention to the value of nature and take fewer risks when dealing with environmental issues – to become more environmentally aware – this suggests that there are both a number of possibilities and difficulties within the broad frame of reference presented by sustainable development. There are of course many reasons for having such a broad approach, and the more this is realised and

---

1   See chapter two and Naess (1973).

59

accepted, the more it will increase the benefits towards any commitment to the environmental perspective. On the other hand, though, there is a risk with the broad claims of sustainable development as it embraces the entire spectrum of social development, and the fact that it has many supporters. It is argued that a cause that touches upon everything, and is the concern of all people, is in danger of not having any influence at all because nobody feels that it is their personal responsibility to act. This is an important reason as to why it is necessary that people should be allowed to develop a basic knowledge of sustainable development e.g. in schools, and there should be the opportunity to absorb the perspectives to such an extent that they become visible both in daily life and in public debate.

What, then, is the present situation, in the beginning of the third millennium, with regard to humankind's relationship with nature and the environment? We can first of all remind ourselves of the extraordinary advancement of technology (chapter one), which has resulted in the fact that, in a modern western industrialised nation, only a few percent of the population are directly involved with producing food from the natural environment e.g. farming, fishing and hunting.

It is also true to say that following a successive expansion from the commitment to preserve and conserve special locations in the environment, we now have a situation where natural resources and environmental issues are generally regarded as being of great significance to the future development of society as a whole. Simultaneously, in industrialised countries many of the more tangible environmental problems have, to a certain extent at least, been dealt with – such as eutrophication of lakes and rivers due to polluted water from industries and urban areas, and dead forests due to smoke and other toxic emissions from nearby factories. But, in many of the most urgent issues concerning sustainable development there seems to be a deterioration rather than an improvement, e.g. the unfair distribution of global resources or the high consumption of fossil fuels.

Throughout this chapter we will address a number of characteristics that we believe are representative of the current natural resource and environmental issues. This will be our way of 'testing the waters', to see what the various opinions and standpoints are on these subjects, as well as looking into the types of perspectives that one has to relate to when working with education for sustainable development.

From Locally Concentrated to Globally Diffuse

Most of the environmental problems during the 20th Century have been 'local and concentrated', e.g. in the form of factory emissions. It has often been possible to link the resulting dead forests and dead fish directly to toxic discharges. On some occasions it has been possible to illustrate on a map how the emissions from a particular industrial area have affected the local environment. But current environmental problems are often more diffuse and span entire regions; even the entire planet. Focus is more on e.g. nitrogen emissions from agricultural land or vehicle exhaust fumes rather than the emissions from a single factory. Similarly, there is more focus on, for instance, the Baltic Sea or the Earth's atmosphere than on a particular lake or river.

One of most serious current environmental issues is the increasing greenhouse effect (the strengthened trapping of solar heat in the planet's atmosphere, just like a very large scale greenhouse, effecting climate and weather). This has become much more 'effective' due to the increase in greenhouse gases created by human activity. The main greenhouse gas is carbon dioxide and the atmospheric quantity has been steadily increasing ever since humans began to use fossil fuels (coal, oil and natural gas). This type of environmental issue has rather diffuse links to emission and effect. The actual *mechanisms* are often very complicated and the geographical *scale* is very large – in the case of the greenhouse effect it is global.

The more traditional, concentrated and local environmental problems could often be experienced first hand out in the landscape. For example, it was possible to take a school class on a field trip to see examples of environmental damage. Whereas nowadays most people in the industrialised countries are aware of the greenhouse effect, very few can claim to have 'experienced it'. This development has resulted in changes in the roles of experts and even science itself. Previous assignments for experts involved determining how much of a particular chemical/toxin could be released into the environment (limit restrictions). This was then followed up with purification measures, taking specimens and issuing regulations in order to make sure that the limits were being observed. In the cases of the more large-scale environmental issues, the role of the experts is often quite simply to attempt to convince people that these problems actually exist. Also here it is important to note that the driving force behind all branches of science is the fact that each individual case is open to critical examination and discussion. This is the reason why there are rarely any unequivocal statements from the experts, which in many cases leaves the general public with the difficult choice of deciding on the credibility of the reports. In today's society, there are a great many threats and hazards, which are also vague and difficult to interpret.[2]

When teaching on the subject of the environment it was often possible, with traditional environmental problems, to 'measure' the extent of the damage by field trips. However the large-scale and diffuse environmental issues are abstract and must be first discussed and defined. There is also the additional aspect, as in the case of large-scale environmental damage, of the fact that the results often affect remote places and times.There can be situations where one must be able to relate to threats such as the possibility of excessive exhaust emissions in Europe resulting in the low lying countries in South East Asia being completely flooded in just a few decades.

From Industrial Emissions to Industrial Production

Although current environmental problems can be experienced as being vague and geographically remote, they are simultaneously often directly linked with our everyday consumption and lifestyles. We could, for example, compare the difference between travelling by car and adding to the greenhouse effect, or going by train, which

2   For an overview of the discussions on the 'risk society' see chapter six.

with hydroelectric energy can operate without releasing carbon dioxide into the atmosphere. Or, we could compare a conventionally grown bunch of bananas with fair trade bananas in the supermarket; in all likelihood the cheapest, conventionally grown bananas are produced without any regard to 'economical, social or ecological sustainability'. On the contrary, the conventional bananas (or coffee, chocolate etc.) will probably have been produced under conditions that are injurious to the land, the workers and the surrounding environment. This is in contrast to ecologically produced bananas that, hopefully, have been produced by using non-toxic or alternative biocides and by people with a high level of social responsibility – and therefore will probably be more expensive as the production process was geared to objectives other than merely producing large and cheap bananas.

Now that environmental and resource issues are increasingly concerned with industrial (including agricultural) production as compared with the previous focus on toxic emissions, there is also an awareness that these issues affect the private economies and consumer habits of the general public. For example, what is an acceptable price for a bunch of bananas at your local supermarket?

The attention that is now given to different types of produce also leads to attention being drawn to the products' respective origin and recycling into the ecosystem, or what kinds of raw materials are used in the production of a certain product, and what happens to these items when they no longer fulfil a purpose (when they have become 'refuse'). By using this perspective, we can gain an understanding of concepts such as 'life cycle assessment' and 'product responsibility' that allow an insight into the entire production process of a given product. What arrives and leaves through a factory's gates is nowadays, from an environmental viewpoint, considered just as important as what is discharged from its chimneys and drains.

From the perspective of education for sustainable development, this implies that the daily activities of every single person are extremely relevant. It is possible to investigate practically any product on sale, and with the help of product organisations and environmental certifications, gain some insight into the economical, social and ecological effects that are caused by various consumer choices.

Environmental Problems as International Trade

What has become of the 'old' environmental issues from factory sewers and chimneys? Have these problems been solved? The answer is unfortunately no, and even in high-income nations there are still a large number of these problems to deal with. There are also a great many urgent cases in the low-income countries of the world. Additionally, we should not forget for a moment that even though the standard of living in the world is on the increase, there are still areas where standards are getting worse, and the divide between the rich and poor is growing dramatically (i.e. an increasing level of relative poverty). We see increasing economical contrasts between countries and between different groups of people within countries.[3] Aside from the injustices involved in these circumstances, the increasing economic and resource divide is also the cause of increasing national security problems. The vastly disproportionate resource distribution apparent in the world today, is a main priority of sustainable development.

Whilst on the topic of these differences between the high- and low-income regions of the world, it is important to point out that in the 'third world', the environmental and resource problems are often cases of resource depletion, in the form of e.g. reduced water tables, deforestation, soil erosion and loss of top soil.[4] In addition to this there is a catalogue of environmental and resource problems which can be directly linked with the unfair relationship that exists between the high-income nations (including trans-national corporations) and the low-income nations of the world. One example is the movement of production from a high-income to a low-income country in order to avoid environmental legislation in the home country, and where the high-income nations then import the goods at a much cheaper price – ignoring the hazards involved for both the employees and the environment in the production country. Another example of global dumping is when transport ships

3   For further reading see the yearbooks *The State of the World*.
4   See yearbooks *The State of the World*.

and other vessels fit for the scrap-yard are sent to low-income countries for 'deconstruction'. The previously mentioned import of tropical fruit or coffee is yet another illustration of this type of problem that could lead to environmental damage.

A final and more long-term aspect that should be mentioned here concerns the issues that surround biotechnology and the strong interest from the agribusiness sector of imposing patents on genetic material from the low-income countries. This could mean that the low-income regions of the world sell off the genetic heritage of their natural environment, e.g. different types of plant or a specific characteristic of a plant, to large multinational corporations – which will most likely be repurchased (probably at a very high price) and used in agricultural production.

From State Control to Local Planning, Trans-national Agreements and Market Solutions

Although international influences have been essential aspects in conservation and environmental issues during the 20th Century, many issues have been addressed on a national level. Pressure groups, authorities, legislation, management and the influencing of public opinion have usually been concerned with just one country. However, mainly due to the developments which have been already discussed – both globally and locally – the following will be a presentation on the local and trans-national perspective which will be introduced both as a complement to and sometimes as an alternative to the national standpoint.

In the case of the local outlook, the work that followed 'Agenda 21' (the agenda for the 21st Century that was agreed upon at the 1992 UN conference in Rio de Janeiro) is probably one of the clearest examples. In this plan of action for sustainable development, it was clearly emphasised that the need for 'grass roots' engagement through the commitment of local government, education and various NGOs was essential. In a country such as Sweden, Agenda

21 manifests itself in the form of influencing public opinion, education and social adaptation on a local level and in accordance with sustainable development.

The growing globalised character of environmental and natural resource problems, referred to earlier, indicates the need for an increase in trans-national agreements and conditions. The fact that, in the conventional sense, an international legislative body does not exist (an equivalent to a national parliament) means that the international level is dependent on individual agreements which all countries are encouraged to follow. In brief, these meetings consist of many countries, with varying political agendas, being represented at a large conference, where it is hoped that some sort of plan of action can be agreed upon. Whether or not these agreements will be observed is later on decided in the parliaments of each respective country.

Another notable element of environmental policy has been an increased interest in economic means of control and market solutions. Through adjustments in taxation levels or fees, it is possible to stimulate the production and consumption of environmentally friendly products. For example, some work has been done to try to eliminate the use of leaded petrol. However, contrary to the more conventional methods of using legislation and official watchdogs to enforce regulations and deadlines for when engines, fuel stations and motorists are to make the change to unleaded fuel, the automobile industry itself has a major responsibility for introducing the necessary changes. A major motivating factor is, of course, the economic adjustments enforced by the authorities making unleaded petrol cheaper, relatively, that will stimulate the respective economies of those involved (buying and selling petrol and cars).

There are many examples where economic measures can probably be an effective way of directing the development of society in a more sustainable direction. Although it is important to remember that in the case of many types of environmental problems, it can be difficult and involve exhaustive negotiations including unavoidable bureaucracy before an agreement is reached on the 'right price'. Of course there are also many environmental issues that are not easily reduced to a question of economics, e.g. the interest of beautiful landscapes to which there is unrestricted access. But, environmental economics, ecological economics and other terms

66

to represent the clash between ecological values and economical values will continue to be widespread in future environmental discussions. The perception of 'growth' and how the growth of society should be measured is one of the most pressing issues here, just as it was in the alternative discussions that took place during the 1970s.[5]

Environmental Commitment: From Words to …?

The previous chapter depicted the development of environmentalism during the 20th Century. It was also emphasised that environmental awareness had successively expanded in scope and depth. With this in mind, it is possible to adopt the idea that this trend will continue to develop in the future – that more and more people will become more and more deeply environmentally engaged. This, of course, is far from being assured, partly due to the fact that current and future environmental issues are often regarded as being diffuse and abstract as was discussed earlier. But it is also important not to disregard the possibility of environmental issues, as has happened to others, being sidelined as a 'verbal parenthesis' in the debates to come. For example, in approximately 10–20 years people may be forced to concede that although the interest in environmental and natural resource issues grew during the 1970s and saw a further expansion in the 1980s, it didn't really become an integral element in social development. Might it be that during the early part of the 21st Century, environmental commitment unfortunately waned and was ultimately superseded by other more pressing social issues?

Nevertheless, there is a great deal of involvement in these issues that suggests that such a pessimistic view of the future commitment to sustainable development is not quite so necessary. For example, the issues have maintained a central position in debates for a sustained period and an increasing amount of 'structural' changes have been made which would be difficult to reverse (certain methods of waste disposal, planning, housing etc.). However, the possi-

---

5   See chapter two, and with regard to environmental economics chapter seven.

bility of a reduction in environmental commitment is already being discussed. And as was mentioned in chapter one of this book, it is a fact that environmental improvements in production and consumption can be negated by the overall increase of production and consumption. This is all the more reason to believe that we are now in a critical period, especially when it means committing to and practicing sustainable development . The question thus remains: is the commitment strong enough to cope with increased costs, a certain amount of discomfort and periods of dissatisfaction when initial attempts prove unsuccessful?

More and More a Question of Attitudes and Ethics

Many earlier environmental problems could, to a large extent, be understood as being technical or scientific (even though their causes were in actual fact societal and developmental issues). This implied – and it still applies – that scientists and technicians could often give reasonable and accurate recommendations as to emission limitations, as well as being able to suggest what type of technical measures should be implemented, e.g. in purification techniques.

But, how is an expert to answer questions such as, e.g., how much aviation fuel can reasonably be used by people taking package tours (or eco adventure holidays) to foreign countries? The strictest of environmentalists may answer 'none at all', due to that fact that it is a non-renewable fossil resource which our generation has already used too much of, not to mention the resulting increased greenhouse effect. The neo liberalist, however, may respond by saying 'as much as possible', as it stimulates global, economic growth and allows for increased opportunities for the research and development of e.g. a better environmentally adapted tourist industry. A third party might suggest that aviation fuel could be used to a certain extent, but only on the condition that it is done in moderation, and if in combination with moral responsibility, in line with global understanding and the practice of consuming experiences rather than material goods.

Current wide-ranging and intangible environmental issues often have no clear scientific explanations in themselves. It is more a question of values and how the world is perceived. What about one's opinion of the responsibilities of the future generations and inhabitants of remote places? What about one's perception of the technical abilities and potential of humankind (e.g. what about the hope of discovering improved energy sources in the future or by applying advanced technology to cope with the environmental damage caused in this age)?

The fact that current and future environmental issues appear to include far reaching cultural implications which touch upon ethics, existential and humanistic viewpoints involves both opportunities and difficulties for the subject of education in sustainable development. On the one hand, it is quite clear that the concept of a sustainable development does not only concern the natural and social sciences and technical developments, but also includes areas within humanities such as history, philosophy and religion. On the other hand, this increase in scope and detail can result in many people feeling unsure of these new perspectives; one could almost anticipate the question 'what happened to nature studies?' It is a risk that earlier environmentally engaged teachers whose main points of reference are in the fields of science, technical engineering or geography, may feel that these new issues might not be relevant to them. But, there is also the fact that many professional groups e.g. teachers who have never previously seen any reason to be engaged in environmental and natural resource questions now feel involved in these issues. If sustainable development is to be taken seriously we can, from an educational point of view, also see this as a dramatic increase in the opportunities for subject integration, theme studies and teamwork.

The 'Instant Society Within Walls'

The first three chapters of this book have outlined how current environmental and natural resource issues are parts of a longer environmental history. There is reason to believe that, even today, these issues not only affect the more tangible aspects of people's lives, but also give rise to questions of a more existential nature. There has also been an account of how humankind's relationship towards nature has changed through time, as well as the practical utilisation of the earth's resources becoming more intense and widespread. Even though history provides a necessary frame of reference for the environmental challenges of our age, there are still new situations and problems where previous experience cannot supply all the answers. To 'regress' – which many critics of environmentalism claim would be the result of any suggested measures – is of course neither possible nor desirable.

One-way of describing the ecological situation from a humane point of view in this late-industrial society is to say that we live in an 'instant society within walls'. A society in which all fundamental links to the ecosystem (water, heating, air conditioning, human and household waste etc.) are either made through walls or underground, by means of water pipes, heating systems, ventilations systems, sewerage pipes, electrical cables etc. We have constructed a technical living space – literally within walls – that consists of housing, schools, office space and industrial areas in which we spend most of our lives. The floors are our ground, the roofs our limit and protection, and the various cables, pipes and transport systems sustain our biological functions. The additional fact that both money and commodities such as milk and news etc. are accessed through holes, hatches, cables and screens in walls only makes the depiction clearer. As we already know, we do not need to go back too many generations to find a situation where the majority of people had to go literally out-of-doors in order to obtain firewood, drinking-water and food, not to mention to perform bodily functions.

'Doors in the Walls of the Instant Society'

Today's 'instant society within walls' holds one of the most fundamental challenges for environmental education and education for sustainable development of our time. It is literally about opening the doors in the walls of our instant society to the outdoors. With the help of field trips and education in the landscapes of the outdoors we can then create a deeper awareness of the past and present state of our instant society, by referring to history, geography, biology, drama, language, ecology, mathematics etc. . By opening these doors of our instant society, a thorough understanding could be established both of the great technical ability and organisational capacity of humans , as well as humankind's vulnerability, relationship with nature and dependency on the environment.

Here there is every reason to benefit from the inspiration received from the traditions of movements going out-of-doors of the 'instant' society. These movements have been an important undercurrent during the development of the industrial society. As was discussed in the previous chapter, during the last 150 years people have been taking part in outdoor pursuits and recreational activities in various ways. Even though many of the characteristics of the industrial society are also inherent in many of these activities – achievement, competition, technology and commercialisation – there has also been a significant amount of seeking 'alternative lifestyles' other than those characterised by industrial society. With perspectives influenced by Romanticism and more recent alternative movements there have been a desire to find a more 'natural' and 'simple' lifestyle, with a particular preference for landscapes such as coastal regions, mountains and forests, where nature is perceived to be present in a very tangible way.[6]

As this book focuses on the environment, children and youth, it is of particular interest to bring to the foreground (sometimes critically) a number of tendencies in the current approaches towards outdoor life and nature based tourism. Examples of what seem to be increasingly important aspects are: eco-tourism (with more or less far reaching ambitions of environmentalism), the expanding grey area between outdoor life and sports (e.g. multi sports), and the globalisation of outdoor recreational space (the fact that suitable locations are sought out all over the world in order to suit a particular activity).

Traditional aspects, such as the availability of natural landscapes and green areas in and around urban districts, represent important

6   See further in e.g. Schmitt (1969) and Nash (1982). In Swedish see Sandell & Sörlin (2000).

'doors' in our instant society, which, from the perspectives of education for sustainable development, are important to preserve and encourage an awareness of. Something that is not always included in the discussions on the necessity of greener school facilities and raising awareness of outdoor life in schools is physical planning (e.g. the possibility of being able to cycle to school and the existence of 'green' environments for children to play). However, it is also important to emphasise the fact that the transition from out-of-doors to a deeper environmental commitment, along the lines laid down by sustainable development, is neither clear nor easy. It is, of course, a matter of *how* people are outdoors, e.g. *where* they are, *what* they are doing, *who* they are with and *what* methods/approaches of understanding are applied etc.

In addition, looking at how you relate to your own human body as a means of relating to nature can, in a deeper sense, be linked with the idea of 'doors' out through the walls of the instant society. In other words, we can regard the human body as a fascinating example of that which we can, to some extent, control – such as moving and talking and that which we have no control of – such as the beating of our heart, ageing etc.).[7] Another important 'door' which represents an in-depth look at current society's relationship with the environment is to allow oneself to be inspired to seek the meditative, non material aspects of life instead of immediately embracing everything which falls into the categories of: 'civilisation' and 'progress'. One example is that outdoor recreation makes it possible to experience 'something other' than the viewpoints, values and material settings of industrial society. This means – in line with the above section 'More and More a Question of Attitudes and Ethics'–looking for the potential of out-of-doors as a educational tool for highlighting the qualities of lifestyles which are a little slower, a lot quieter and that suggest a much more humble presence in this cosmic house in which we live.[8]

---

7   Compare with our definition of 'nature' in chapter one.
8   This addresses e.g. outdoor life as an education for sustainable development in accordance with a deep ecological 'alternative' development perspective such as the terminology used in this book (see e.g. Reed & Rothenberg, 1993).

Further Reading

The State of the World is an annual environmental report from the World Watch Institute in Washington that is translated and issued in many countries around the world. It gives accurate and comprehensive information on the environment, global distribution and future perspectives. Each report includes general overviews as well as different chapters on e.g. energy, transportation, agriculture etc. that allows for an detailed overview of various global situations by looking at reports from previous years. In the case of 'doors in the instant society' there are surveys of the social phenomena outdoor recreation and nature based tourism, such as Robert E. Manning's *Studies in Outdoor Recreation: Search and Research for Satisfaction* (Oregon State Univ. Press, 1999), with a focus on children *Children and Nature: Psychological, Sociocultural, and Evolutionary Investigations* (Kahn, Jr. P.H. & Kellert, S.R. Eds., The MIT Press, 2002) and more practically oriented literature such as *Teaching in the Outdoors* (Hammerman, R. & Hammerman M., Interstate Printers and Publishers, 1985) or Joseph Cornell's *Sharing the Joy of Nature: Nature Activities for All Ages* (Dawn Publications, 1989); or in Swedish, *Friluftslivets pedagogik: För kunskap, känsla och livskvalitet* (The Pedagogy of Outdoor Life: For Knowledge, Feeling and Quality of Life by Britta Brügge; Matz Glantz & Klas Sandell (Eds.), (Liber, 2002.)

Other Reference Literature

Naess, Arne (1973). The Shallow and the Deep, Long-Range Ecology Movement: A Summary. *Inquiry*, Vol. 16, pp. 95–100.

Nash, Roderick (1982/1967). *Wilderness and the American Mind* (3rd edition). New Haven and London: Yale University Press.

Reed, Peter & Rothenberg, David (Eds.) (1993). *Wisdom in the Open Air: The Norwegian Roots of Deep Ecology*. London: University of Minnesota Press, Minneapolis.

Sandell, Klas & Sörlin, Sverker (Eds.) (2000). *Friluftshistoria – från 'härdande friluftslif' till ekoturism och miljöpedagogik: Teman i det svenska friluftslivets historia* (The history of outdoor recreation – from 'the tough outdoor life' to eco tourism and environmental pedagogy: Themes in Swedish outdoor history). Stockholm: Carlssons bokförlag.

Schmitt, Peter J. (1969). *Back to Nature: The Arcadian Myth in Urban America*. New York: Oxford University Press.

The previous three chapters gave an overview of humankind's development from hunter-gatherer to today's industrial society. Throughout the years humankind has successively transformed and utilised the natural environment on an ever-increasing scale. Nowadays, our relationship with the natural environment is discussed in terms of sustainable development, environmental issues, and environmental and sustainable education.

Part II will take on a more in depth focus on environmental problems by presenting four different perspectives on environmental and resource issues. We will first of all present a natural science-based perspective on the essence of nature. Most of the focus will be on ecology – the branch of science that has possibly contributed most to our present understanding of current environmental issues. However, even knowledge-based debates on our correlation with the natural environment are nowadays usually characterised by questions of values. In chapter five we will therefore address humankind's relationship with nature as a question of values, and we will consider various environmentally ethical options and environmentally moral correlations. The environmental ethics that we form make up the basis for our individual approach to environmental problems, e.g. how we act as consumers. But in the development of a future society, it is also necessary to develop a collective responsibility where the actions of individuals are limited – but still made possible – through a process of legislation and economic regulation. To illustrate this further, chapter six will introduce a discussion with a view to forming political perspectives on environmental issues with a clear emphasis on the democratic aspects. The last of these four chapters presenting different perspectives (chapter seven) will highlight the economic aspects. In particular, environmental economics will be discussed as an example of a tool to be used with regard to the implementation of a sustainable development.

These four perspectives on environmental problems – natural science-based, value-based, politically-based and based on environmental economics – are examples of central view-points of how we understand, discuss and act upon our current association with the natural environment. These perspectives illustrate some of the common points of departure that influence our ability to answer questions such as: What is an environmental problem? What are the necessary skills required to deal with environmental problems? What should be done about them? The answers to these questions – which perspective one takes – have a great deal of influence on teaching in these areas. This later forms the basis for a discussion in Part III, which address how environmental and resource issues could be approached in schools.

4 Environmental Problems from an Ecological Point of View

What is a Lake?

If we imagine ourselves standing on a shore overlooking a lake in e.g. Scandinavia, what do we actually see?

- Possibly a transitory geological anomaly. A small pool on of the face of the earth formed by the previous establishment of mountain chains and the impact of inland ice. The lake will probably later transform into marshland and eventually to dry land due to the natural erosion process that level out the earth's surface until the next large-scale geographical transformation.
- Or perhaps we see the lake as a habitat[1] for a certain population[2] in which we have an interest. Questions raised might include: Why do perch stop growing and then continue to live for years and years without increasing in size? How does the perch function as a species and is this particular lake a suitable environment to carry out this type of study?
- We might instead regard the lake as an ecosystem – with its boundaries being the lake shore or its catchment area – with a diversity of species in the air and the ground as well as the water, which in various ways interrelate with each other and with the environment with regard to material resources and energy. Or we may perhaps choose to see the lake as a microcosm of the large ecosystem of the whole world.
- The lake could perhaps instead be seen as a collection place for nutrients from nearby high production agriculture. What we then see is anthropogenic environmental damage[3] due to an

1   The natural environment in which a certain species lives.
2   All the individuals of a certain species within a certain area.
3   A change in the environment caused by humans that is perceived as negative.

excess of nutrients which results in the water in the lake being clouded by plankton and which eventually, runs out into the sea through the river system, causing increased algal blooms which in turn leads to problems for marine vegetation necessary for fish reproduction, which leads to ....

All these perspectives of a lake share the common factor of being characterised by ecology and other natural sciences. This is in contrast to seeing the lake as a place of, for example, inspirational beauty for poetry and painting; an example of God's omnipotence; a recreational resort for swimming, sunbathing and fishing; or the subject of a disputation of ownership with all the economical and legal implications.

Ecology is a natural science-based view of knowledge that has its origins in the 19th Century, although it didn't receive any great attention until the environmental debates began in the industrialised nations after the Second World War. From the 1970s onwards, many school children have mainly seen the environment and humankind's relationship with it according to terms originating in ecology like material cycling, diversity, energy, food chains etc.

This perspective will be the frame of reference in the following text and based on the general views of the natural sciences, with particular focus on environmental problems in the industrialised nations.

Current Ecology – Two main Perspectives

Ecology is a branch of biology. The word ecology comes from the Greek *oikos* – house, and *logos* – a study of, i.e. the study of the house. The word 'house' can here be understood to represent the totality that in which all things live. A common definition of ecology is: a study of the relationship of organisms to one another and to their physical surroundings. Early ecology was mainly interested in the study of the influence of environmental factors on individual organisms. However in the 1950s, the Odum brothers[4] developed

---

4   Eugene and Howard Odum, American ecologists who have had a great deal of influence within ecological research (see Worster, 1994).

an interest for the more large-scale processes that contributed to the entire system in the natural world. Thereafter ecology developed into two fields: *population ecology,* which further developed the earlier study of individuals and *systems ecology,* which focuses on entire ecosystems.

Below we will outline a more detailed study of the viewpoints of population and systems ecology and continue with sections on transformation, biological diversity and human involvement. The chapter concludes with a discussion on the relationship between ecological knowledge and the various options available for the development of society.

Population Ecology

Population ecology mainly deals with the study of the changes in populations and how they interact with each other. In this context, *population* means all the individuals of a species that inhabit a specific area, e.g. all the perch in a lake.

The size of a population is influenced by factors both within the population and the level of interaction with populations of other species. This relationship can have both positive and negative implications for the growth of a population. One of the most important influencing factors is *competition.* Within a species there can be competition for food, partners, nesting space etc. A way of avoiding competition within a species is to divide an area into territories, which gives a better chance of providing food for the young. The competition between species is mainly about food and habitat. As a result of this, the different species develop separate *niches*: they diversify themselves in terms of *what* they eat, or *when* they eat, or *where* they eat.

Certain species develop a *symbiosis* (a mutually advantageous relationship between species) e.g. there is a symbiosis between many types of mushroom and certain types of tree. Certain populations can also have a *predator-prey* relationship, as with wolves and deer. This means that the number of wolves is dependent on the availability of food i.e. the number of deer determines the number of wolves. However the deer population is affected by other factors, such as whether or not the conditions are favourable – e.g. a mild winter allows for an increased availability for food – whereas the number can be drastically reduced during a particularly harsh winter (these changes then also affect the wolf population).

This dynamic state between the populations results in the fact that interaction between species affects the growth of populations, leading to the constant fluctuation in the number of individuals within the species.

The term *carrying capacity* of an environment is used to describe its suitability for the long-term survival of a population therein. If the capacity (which of course can be changed, for instance due to changes in climate) is exceeded, then one or more restricting factors emerge – for example in the form of a shortage of food or water, or loss of nesting space.

Interaction both within and between the species puts pressure on the individuals means that those which can best adapt to the demands of the surrounding environment have the best chances of survival and consequently the survival of their genes. This *selection pressure* is the most important aspect of evolution, and is present throughout the natural world. The mechanisms of evolution have resulted in numerous adaptations. One just needs to reflect on TV's nature documentaries that often focus on the extraordinary abilities of e.g. animals to change colour according to the immediate environment, birds which can extract insects from tree trunks with the help of a twig, butterflies and moths with large 'eyes' on their wings etc.

Systems Ecology

As we have seen, different species interact with each other. But plants and animals also interact with the *abiotic* (nonliving) surroundings. Together these interactions result in:

1. An energy flow through plants and animals.
2. A cycle of materia from the abiotic environment through the bodies of living organisms and finally returning to the abiotic environment.

A combination of the living organisms and their abiotic environment make up an *ecosystem*. The study of this system's composition and function is called systems ecology.

Sunlight is the energy source which supports the ecological system. Of all the living organisms, plants and algae have the capacity to utilise sunlight. Through the process of *photosynthesis,* plants can process sunlight into chemical energy which is stored in roots, leaves and seeds etc. In this way the sun's energy becomes available to other organisms. Due to the potential of plants to create energy rich chemical compounds they are termed as *producers,* and the animal life that uses the plants – by eating them or eating other animals (which eat plants) are termed as *consumers.* The majority of the energy intake of animals is expended in the metabolic process, which enables them to be active and, for instance, look for more food or escape from predators. In this process the energy is converted once again, this time into heat which is released into the atmosphere. This is what is meant by an energy flow through the ecosystem.

The energy which is not used during activity is either excreted or stored in the animal e.g. in the form of muscle or fat. It is this stored energy which is available to carnivorous animals. The energy which is present in excrement and in dead plants and animals is processed by *detritivores* e.g. worms, fungi and bacteria, which transform the remaining solar energy to heat.

The flow of energy through the ecosystem thus takes place through the process of animals eating each other. A *food chain* indicates the order in which species eat one another. Each food chain starts with plants or algae. The different levels within the food chain are termed *trophic levels*. In an eco system, the various food chains are interlinked in complex *food webs*.

Since energy is only introduced to the ecosystem via plant life, and animals constantly use energy which is lost in the form of heat, the higher up the food chain a species finds itself the less energy there is to utilise. For each trophic level approximately 90% of the energy is expended in the form of heat. The amount of *biomass* (the total quantity or weight of organisms in a given area) is reduced at each trophic level and this is usually illustrated by a *pyramid of biomass*. In a forest there is much less biomass in voles than there is in the plants which the voles eat, and even less in the foxes which eat the voles. Seen in total, the plant life and algae constitute 99% of all the biomass on earth.

The solar energy that sustains the ecosystem is supplied in a constant flow,[5] but the matter that constitutes the living organisms is limited, and elements such as carbon, phosphorus and nitrogen must therefore be constantly recycled. The elements have differing *cycles*, however, and the governing principle is that they are absorbed by plant life from the earth, water or atmosphere. They are then transferred to animals, which in turn eat the plants, and it is only when the detritivores break down the excrements and dead plants and animals that the matter becomes available to the plant life.

Populations which constitute an ecosystem make up a *community*. Each community is in a state of constant change; some species disappear while others emerge. This series of transformations within a community is referred to as *succession*. For example, if we imagine that we create an area of open ground, it does not take long before easily dispersed, annual plants will appear (in gardens or farmland these are referred to as weeds). After a few years have passed, the weeds will be replaced by more competitive species such as common flowering plants. Later still trees will have grown, casting shade on the ground which results in the ground level flora consisting only of species which can survive in the shade. These various stages of the succession of the vegetation create different conditions for the animals in the area, and therefore the succession also results in changes in the composition of the fauna. A theory within systems ecology is that the ecosystem will eventually reach a final phase. This stage in the succession has been appropriately termed the *climax community*. This stage is considered to be a stable, yet dynamic, relationship between organisms and the surrounding environment.

Stability and Transformation

The changing of the seasons is a distinct natural event in most parts of the world. It is also an event which most people are accustomed to and regard as being part of everyday life. In the above, we dis-

---

5   Even though the sun is estimated to burn out in approximately 5 billion years.

cussed how the number of individuals within their respective populations are in a state of constant change, as well as how an ecosystem can undergo a so-called succession. Also relevant is the fact that life on earth is being transformed, in the long term, by climate change and evolution. New species find new niches or become better adapted to new conditions and replace other species that either become extinct or migrate. Fluctuations in sunlight, volcanic eruptions, meteorite impacts and geological transformations such as tectonic movement and inland ice also change the conditions for living organisms in the long-term perspective.

These perspectives remind us of the fact that nothing in nature is permanent. Everything is in constant motion, from mountains and continents, to species, the climate and the seasons. At the same time it is also apparent that a certain resistance to change is a determining attribute in the natural world.

The laws of *thermodynamics* can be interpreted to the effect that disorder is much more likely than order (if we throw the pieces of a jigsaw puzzle into the air it is unlikely that the pieces will fall to the ground as a complete puzzle). Therefore everything in life is inevitably heading towards disorder and decay (for many people it is enough to think of the tidy/untidy desk scenario). In light of this, *life* can be seen as an amazing process that perpetually struggles against the current and establishes and maintains order and structure. When an organism (established order) dies, the process of decay (disorder) begins immediately. The sun's energy is necessary in order to carry out the establishment of order among disorder, as are the complex life forms that have evolved for billions of years.

The natural selection process has favoured the life processes in all species which, in various ways, protect their bodies, their offspring and their food supply, as well as their avoidance of various threats, such as bacteria, predators etc. Even the ecosystem can be said to compensate for changes e.g. in the event of climate change the populations of the ecosystem undergo changes in that species become extinct and others emerge as well as population adjustments taking place within existing species.

This relationship between stability and transformation in the short and long term is essential to the understanding of how the natural world functions. It is, however, important to point out that there is no consensus among researchers as to the exact function of the ecosystem. Some ecologists claim that nature is best understood as a totality based on the mutual dependence between the species. According to this viewpoint, each species must ensure its own survival, but in such a way as to benefit the totality of the whole system. In this sense the ecosystem can be seen as a super organism with the ability to adapt and control itself in exactly the same way as other organisms. Based on this viewpoint, the study of human ecology has therefore reached the conclusion that humans should interfere with the natural environment as little as possible.

Other ecologists claim that, in practice, it is difficult to ascertain any kind of consistent, stable and harmonious order in the natural world. Therefore the existence of any definite climax communities (see the above section: systems ecology) with complete stability has been questioned. This has led to some researchers in ecology adopting the approach that the natural environment is unpredictable and the different aspects of the ecosystem are altogether more loosely connected and temporary. A theoretical basis for this approach to the natural world can be found in the chaos theory. With the help of computer simulations, it has been demonstrated that even the smallest of events can have quite dramatic consequences for the system as a whole. Another theory which is central to current ecology is the complexity theory, which sees nature as constantly creating variable patterns in which the same constituents are reorganised in different ways. This implies that the natural world is infinitely more complicated than was previously thought, and any long-term predictions are, therefore, simply not possible.

The discussion between the different ecological stand points has given rise to a number of important questions in the environmental debate: if there is no kind of harmonious ecological balance in the natural world which humankind can disturb, how are we to relate to the changes which humankind makes in the environment?[6]

Another disputed question is how we should relate to biological diversity. The term *diversity* usually refers to the number of species and how large their respective populations are within an ecosystem. An earlier understanding was that a high level of diversity

6   For further details see a summary of the discussion in Worster (1994). More
     details on new ecology can be found in Botkin (1992), Gleick (1996), and Russek
     (2001).

© The Authors and Studentlitteratur

allowed for an ecosystem with high stability, with the understanding that a large concentration of different species could act as a buffer which would minimize any changes and therefore maintain stability within the ecosystem. If a certain species became extinct, another species would be able to replace it. However, studies in the field have proved this theory to be less than completely airtight. One example is the tropical rain forests which have an extremely high level of biodiversity, but at the same time are relatively susceptible to any outside interference.

A common stand point is, however, that global biodiversity is important, partly because the global ecosystem should be able to adapt to and possibly even resist future environmental fluctuations, and partly because the biodiversity can be seen in terms of evolution's genetic 'capital'. A large biodiversity benefits the circumstances in which life on earth can develop as dynamically as possible. An opposing opinion has held that life on earth could be maintained with only a few species whilst still allowing humankind to continue its present lifestyle. One important remark is, however, that one should not only take what we already know into consideration, but we should also respect that which is unknown, as no one can claim to be in possession of the knowledge and control required to accurately predict any large scale global development.

Natural Transformation and Human Involvement

This book began with the question of whether or not humans are only animals, and this chapter began with the question of what we actually see when we consider a lake from an ecological viewpoint. Between these two questions on humankind's relationship to the natural environment we discover one of ecology's most important questions: what are the differences between natural transformations and transformations caused by human involvement? It was illustrated in the above that the environment is in a state of constant change: certain species are on the increase while others are in decline and some are disappearing altogether; weather systems and the climate as a whole fluctuate constantly in both long and short-

4 Environmental Problems from an Ecological Point of View

term perspectives etc. All the forces of nature mentioned above – evolution, succession and competition – are constantly in action in the environment and contribute to both large and small changes. Many of these events, such as forest fires, locust invasions and storms, can have negative outcomes for humankind. However, we do not label these natural events as being environmental problems, as this term is only used when human involvement has played a conclusive part. We do know, however, that many changes in the environment are the result of direct human involvement and that many of these events have a negative effect on the natural environment as well as on humans themselves – this type of changes can be described as environmental problems (see fig. 1.1). This implies that when we observe changes in the natural environment we must first determine if the developments are either natural or anthropogenic events. There then follows the difficulty in determining whether or not the changes caused by man are positive or negative. For example, if there are very few weeds in a field as a result of modern agriculture, this is generally seen as something positive. If, however, the result of having weed free fields means toxins in food and the reduction in local bird life, then the outcome clearly takes on a number of negative aspects.

The question of the difficulties of determining natural developments and those developments caused by human activity has already been raised. The event in question must firstly be compared with reference examples where human involvement is negligible, and secondly, one must be in possession of all the facts concerning the details of the new event.

If we take the example of climatic changes and the *greenhouse effect* as a pressing environmental issue, we must first have an understanding of how the global climate has changed over long periods and in different locations. These results can be based on e.g. samples taken from inland ice, which can illustrate the natural climate changes of the planet up to many thousands of years ago (during the majority of this period humans had very little impact on the environment). In addition to this we can include our knowledge of the actual process behind the changes e.g. to what extent the earth's climate is affected by carbon dioxide levels, changes in solar activity, volcanic eruptions etc. (these calculations are usually carried out in the form of large scale computer simulations which

© The Authors and Studentlitteratur

include all the factors effecting the climate). If all the available data is collated it is hoped that some sort of satisfactory estimate can be presented, and illustrate the degree to which the climate change has been influenced by humankind during the last century. Current research groups seem to be unanimous that human involvement is today one of the important contributing factors of climate changes, and they can even to some degree estimate the consequences of those changes.

Ecology and the Development of Society

How should the worldview held by ecologists influence the development of society? It is not uncommon that very specific demands are made on how the economy, politics, community planning etc. should be run according to ecological guidelines. When deciding on procedures, experts can often reach an agreement by applying ecological theories. However, all the facts, even those concerning humankind's role in the natural world, must be seen in terms of values before they can be expressed as demands for social development. There can be value questions concerning the capacity of humans to manage complex systems and acquire new skills, or the rights and role of humankind in relation to other species. Ecology can therefore be applied as a basis for a wide range of debates in deciding the most suitable social development strategies.

Ecology is often used as a pretext that society should be adapted to the conditions of the natural environment. The most important reasons for this are ecology's reminders of how complex the ecosystem is, how little we know about how the system actually functions and how it is affected by human activities. Based on these reminders, the necessity of small-scale projects, local solutions and diversity in all aspects of utilizing natural resources is often claimed. Some also maintain that these aims of environmental adaptation must be combined with a conscious promotion of lifestyles which are not totally committed to material gain.

Thus, an ecological perspective can be used to motivate limited human influence, adjusting to local areas, risk reduction etc. Examples of solutions frequently recommended by ecologists include:

- the necessity of minimizing the risks in terms of human involvement in the natural environment;
- the need to ascertain whether or not an activity causes environmental damage before it is applied in practice – instead of the opposite;
- the need to introduce quickly renewable resources of energy and materials such as wood, wind power and bio gas instead of fossil based resources e.g. nuclear energy, petrol and plastics (both petrol and plastics are oil based products) and in addition ensure that all forms of waste products are employed to the greatest extent via refuse recycling etc.;
- the need to limit energy consumption, by both reducing the global population rate and, just as importantly, reducing the northern hemisphere's disproportionate consumption of both matter and energy;
- the need for improved environmental inspections and tests by means of e.g. taking samples, satellite surveillance and ecological research projects.

But ecology can also be used as a pretext that it is necessary to attempt to control the natural environment based on human interests with the help of ecological expertise. From this standpoint, and in an area such as climate change, regardless of whether the changes have been caused by natural or human activity, we should conclusively decide which type of climate we would like on planet Earth and make a serious long term effort to achieve such a goal. An extreme version of this would be the science fiction's world of biospheres – hermetically sealed glass bubbles on Earth. At the opposite end of the scale, in an equally extreme form of adaptation, we would see a low production, (due to trade and industry restrictions) small scale and diversified self-sustaining economy. Ecological expertise and debate will, with all probability, have great importance for both these extremes.

We can illustrate these various options of interpretation with the help of the scientific and ecological perspectives on the lake that were introduced at the beginning of this chapter. One can, for example, ask oneself: do people really need to swim in lakes (there are swimming pools and the lake will become marsh land anyway in the long run); is it necessary to fish in the oceans (this practice can be replaced with regulated fish farms, which function in much the same way as crops are produced in agricultural farming); does it really matter if some species of marine vegetation is dying out (it is not exactly a staple diet of humans)? Or on the contrary, is it that contact with the natural environment, natural beauty, bathing and sailing in lakes and oceans, sustainable professional fishing etc. are all representations of a good quality of life and an important ecological indicator that humankind's basic means of existence is not threatened?

In conclusion: ecological knowledge of how 'natural systems' function and how humankind influences these 'systems' are necessary aspects of the basis for the various decisions on continued social development. However, the ecological knowledge to be placed in the fore ground, how the results are to be interpreted and how they are to be integrated into political decisions are all subject to the scrutiny of values. These aspects of values in problematic environmental issues will be addressed in the following chapters.

Further Reading

Two good examples of literature which address the general principles of ecology are: *Ecology: The experimental analysis of distribution and abundance*, by Charles Krebs (Addison-Wesley Educational Publishers, 2001) and *Ecology: Theories and applications*, by Peter Stiling (Pearson Higher Education, 2001). Further reading about the ecological perspective on the environmental problems of our time can be found in *Ecological Principles and Environmental Issues* by Peter Jarvis (Pearson Higher Education, 2003) and in Eugene Odum's *Ecological Vignettes* (Gordon and Breach, 1998). The new perspectives of ecology are for instance presented in *Discordant Harmonies: A New Ecology for the Twenty-first Century* by Daniel B. Botkin (Oxford University Press, 1992) and in *Environmental Science: Earth as a Living Planet* by Daniel B. Botkin and Edward A. Keller (John Wiley & Sons, 2002).

Other Reference Literature

Worster, Donald (1994). *Nature's Economy: A History of Ecological Ideas.* Cambridge: Cambridge University Press.

Gleick, James (1996) *Chaos: Making a new science.* London: Vintage.

Russek, Janet (Ed.) (2001). *Nature's Chaos.* Boston: Little Brown and Company.

5 Environmental Problems from an Ethical Point of View

A Conflict of Values

Earlier we established that humankind has, throughout the ages, influenced and transformed the natural environment and consequently the conditions governing life for humankind itself and all other living organisms. In the previous chapter we introduced ecology as being the branch of the natural sciences that, possibly more than any other, has contributed to our knowledge of the effects of human influence on the natural environment. Even though there are certain differences of opinion, there is a general consensus among ecologists on the great changes in the environment both in the past and the present. However, there is a lot less consensus in the question of how this ecological expertise is to be applied in the development of standards for how we are to live. Which type of environmental changes are considered acceptable and which are to be classed as problems, how serious they are and what steps should be taken, are all issues in which there is a great deal of debate.

Thus the definition of environmental problems made in chapter one (see fig. 1.1) can, from an ethical point of view, be extended in the following way: environmental problems are transformations that have taken place as a result of human interaction with nature, which is in conflict with certain norms and values. Human beings have different norms and different values. We all have more or less differing opinions about what is important, good, bad, right and wrong in life. Based on this we could say that environmental issues are essentially conflicts of human values and norms; and when dealing with values and norms, the various fields within the scientific world cannot supply any satisfactory answers. In this chapter, we will therefore attempt to depict environmental problems as being questions of values, as well as taking stock of which ethical values lie behind the differing opinions in the environmental debate. We will especially focus on the ethical relationship between man and nature. The purpose of this is to attempt to familiarise ourselves with the number of available alternatives when discussing how we should relate to the natural environment and why we should relate to it in a certain way.

Ethics and Morals

The terms ethics and morals can be understood in different ways. Basically, they have the same meaning but have different origins. Ethics has its etymology in Greek, and moral has it in Latin. In philosophical nomenclature, however the terms have been given slightly different meanings in that *moral* has come to represent our reactions in specific situations and our attitudes towards what is good and bad, or correct and incorrect actions. Morals are accordingly associated with our judgements about how to act and how to relate to our surroundings.

Ethics concern the critical and rational study of norms and values that make up human moral conduct. This can result in a number of interrelated general ethical principles. Ethics therefore does not concern personal gratification, what we prefer, and what we would like to see, but rather values which we *ought to* realise or support due to the consequences of our conduct on other people and nature.[1]

Before we continue with our topic of environmental ethics, a closer look at different values from an ethical point of view is required. An initial division of values into instrumental value, intrinsic value and inherent worth can be made.

Instrumental value has something that can be used as a means of achieving something 'good'. The value is then based on the usefulness of the thing itself. Something that posses instrumental value can be substituted; if we discover something which can more effec-

---

1   This concerns normative ethics and not, for example, descriptive ethics or meta-ethics.

tively achieve the desired result then it automatically has more value and, in all probability, is chosen to replace the original. Money is an example of something that has instrumental value to most of us. In itself it has no value, but it functions as a means of acquiring material objects or experiences that we find desirable.

Intrinsic value has something which is accredited a value in itself, regardless of whether or not it serves as a means of achieving some other or higher value. That which has intrinsic value is considered a goal in itself. Good health is an example of something which is usually considered as having intrinsic value and is therefore a goal which we see as worth reaching; people exercise or eat high fibre diets in order to become healthy. Another example is the United Nation's Declaration of Human Rights, which states that all people have intrinsic values which can not be violated regardless of who that person may be, what they have done and how useful they are deemed to be.

In order to be accredited with intrinsic values, an external evaluator is necessary; it is therefore required that someone appreciates or respects the value in question. Thus, intrinsic value here means: subjective value as a goal in itself. This implies an intrinsic value that is, in some sense, created by people; we allocate intrinsic value. An important question is: according to which criteria is something accredited with intrinsic value? That which has intrinsic value must have one or more qualities that demonstrate how it differs from those objects or concepts that are not considered to have intrinsic value. For example, we might regard a squirrel as having intrinsic value, but not a stone, due to the basic fact that that a squirrel can experience pain and suffering.

However, we can also consider certain things as having values which are objective and eternal, which have always been in existence and that humankind has discovered during its cultural development.[2] This implies that values can exist independent of humankind; collectively, these are sometimes referred to as *inherent worth*.[3] We can, for instance, ask ourselves whether slaves, women and chil-

---

2 Compare with how we reach conclusions – e.g. now that we know that the planet is spherical, we also know it was spherical before we discovered the fact.
3 See Norton, 1987.

dren of the Middle Ages had inherent worth, despite the fact that the Declaration of Human Rights had not then been formulated and accepted. Similarly, we can reflect on whether or not animals have only instrumental value because they are used by humans in various ways, or whether we should accredit them with intrinsic values. It could be possible that the values of animals are natural and independent of humankind i.e. inherent worth.

It is that which has intrinsic value or inherent worth to which we are morally bound and should therefore be considerate towards in our conduct. That which has intrinsic value or inherent worth is said to be *morally relevant.*

Environmental Morals and Environmental Ethics

Environmental morals concern our conduct and relation towards nature in practice. Accordingly, environmental ethics can be said to be the rational and systematic evaluation of our interaction with the natural environment, and subsequently the inquiry into how we ought to relate to the natural world. Environmental ethics can therefore be distinguished from human ethics in that the latter is concerned with the norms and values of actions and relations between people or between people and society.

We have earlier stated that the transformations in nature caused by humans do not always have an immediate or a tangible effect on our lives. It is not possible to detect with our own senses the greenhouse effect, the thinning of the ozone layer, or the diminishing number of species, nor do we suffer to any great extent from these developments. On the contrary, we are afforded many personal advantages by consuming a vast range of luxuries and ignoring all the hard work involved in recycling and other 'eco friendly' activities. A central question in environmental ethics is therefore: *who should we show consideration to when evaluating the consequences of our interaction with nature?*

In a technologically advanced industrialised society, the consequences of our actions have far reaching implications, both in time and space and on all aspects of life for humans, animals and plant life alike. One can take a common situation such as driving a petrol-driven car to work which, as opposed to cycling, contributes to the greenhouse effect, which in turn leads to changing conditions for farming and for the 'natural' ecosystems throughout the world. From another viewpoint, by driving a car and burning fossil fuels one has the benefits of (traffic permitting) a quick, effective and comfortable means of transportation to work. It is possible that by releasing exhaust fumes into the atmosphere we might experience a feeling of guilt, as we are aware of the detrimental effect this has on both people and the natural environment. The result is a conflict of values. The different values are opposed and the question is, to whom or what do we have moral obligations and how far do those obligations stretch?

The question is whether or not our moral obligations encompass:

- all the *people alive* on earth today,
- the future, taking the *future generations* of people into consideration,
- the natural environment and having a sense of responsibility towards *other living organisms,*
- *entire biological systems*, e.g. species, ecosystems and landscapes?

A central aspect of environmental ethics is, therefore, what we regard as being morally relevant or what/who is included within the moral sphere. Below we will look more closely at how one can discuss our moral relation to the natural environment by applying various environmentally ethical standpoints.

Environmental Ethical Categories

A category of environmental ethics involves a systematic, cohesive and consistent way of revising the questions raised in regard to humankind's interaction with nature. There are a number of ways of classifying the various environmentally ethical standpoints. The point of departure for the classification which has been chosen here is: who/what is to be included in the environmentally moral sphere, i.e. who/what do we have a moral responsibility towards and what are the reasons for considering these morally relevant.[4]

Here we will treat three main categories: the *anthropocentric* which regards only humans as being morally relevant; the *biocentric* which includes animals and in some cases plant life within the moral sphere and finally the *ecocentric* which encompasses the entire ecosystem within its ethical standpoint. Each of these categories has, of course, a number of variations and we will to some extent address the various lines of reasoning within each category respectively.

Anthropocentric Environmental Ethics

In this section we will look into two types of anthropocentric environmental ethics, first, modern anthropocentrism and later a development of this which we have termed late modern anthropocentrism.

Modern Anthropocentrism

The word *anthropos* comes from Greek and means human. The word anthropocentric is used to describe the belief that humankind is at the centre of all existence. *Modern anthropocentricism* can be said to have its origins in the scientific revolution of the 17th Century. The anthropocentric way of regarding humankind's relationship with nature is, therefore, associated with that period in history and it's doctrines of social and cultural development. It is this environmental ethic which formed the basis for the development of the industrialised society.[5]

---

4   This reference point in the division of different orientations of environmental ethics results in the overlooking of other important alternative approaches e.g. ecofeminism which has a gender perspective on environmental ethics and sees ethics as being based on relationships rather than on values (see Merchant, 1980).

5   See chapter two.

The founding idea for modern anthropocentrism is that humankind is seen as being separate from nature. This opinion is based on the dualistic idea that humankind and nature are two great entities. Other aspects include a mechanical and an atomistic view of the natural world: nature is likened to a machine and the individual components are the point of departure in understanding and explaining the world as a whole.

In modern anthropocentric environmental ethics, only humankind is morally relevant. There are two main arguments to support this statement. The first is based on the Christian religion's belief that humankind was created in the image of God. The 17th Century philosopher, René Descartes, developed this further by stating that only humans had souls and were capable of thinking and reasoning. According to Descartes, animals were soulless automatons that also lacked emotions, interests, self-awareness and the ability to experience pain.

The second founding idea originated in the Age of Enlightenment[6] and its belief in human reason and free will. One of the Enlightenment's leading figures, Immanuel Kant, stated that of all the life on earth only humans had the ability to act morally, and that humans are bound, from their knowledge of their duty as rational beings, to obey the categorical imperative to respect other rational beings. This means that only human beings can be included within this moral sphere.

Humankind's unique position allows us the right to rule the natural world, make use of its resources and adapt the natural environment according to our ambitions, desires and interests. The natural world has only instrumental value and its function is to fulfil the wishes of humankind. It is only in this fulfilment that animals, plants, mountains, lakes forests etc are seen as having values.[7]

---

6   The Enlightenment was a philosophical movement formed during the late 18th Century. One of the core beliefs was that humans, through education and applying reason, can distinguish between good and evil, and right and wrong etc., see also chapter six.

7   Compare with how some people can question the rights' of mosquitoes to a life since they are only a source of irritation to humans, but with the realisation that mosquitoes make up part of the diet of small birds, which can be nice to listen to or look at, they can then be granted the right to exist.

In brief, one can say that one of the supporting theories in the modern approach is the strong belief that all of humankind's problems can be solved with the help of science and technology. By investing in scientific and technological development, which can effectively exploit the earth's natural resources, a rapid rate of economical and material growth can be achieved. The modern approach is based, to a large extent, on the optimistic belief that development will solve all present and future problems, i.e. things can only get better!

This also implies that the solutions to environmental problems lie in scientific and technological development. If a natural resource was to become scarce, technological development would then hopefully result in either a more effective way of utilizing the resource or finding another resource as a replacement. This could be interpreted as an example of how the industrialised nations have developed their environmental standpoints based on the original understanding that the planet's natural resources are limitless, as is the planet's capacity to absorb all the waste produced by human activity.

Environmentally ethical demands based on the modern anthropocentric approach are limited in that no humans are to be harmed in the process of extracting and utilizing natural resources. Parallel with the modern approach is also the idea that global resources are divided in a justifiable way. A central question is, therefore, to what extent can this ethical demand be stretched; is it enough that all people have their basic requirements for existence met, or do we all have the right to the same quality of life? However, we do not have to concern ourselves with future generations, as any problems that arise are supposed to be solved through technological development. Neither do we need to care about the natural environment as it only holds instrumental value.

Late-Modern Anthropocentrism

When the effects of the industrialised nations' exploitation of the natural environment became all the more apparent during the second half of the 20th Century, traditional anthropocentric environmental ethics were increasingly disputed. A new anthropocentric ethic began to take shape which questioned certain aspects of modern anthropocentrism's standpoint on nature and humans' relationship with the natural world, but at the same time to a large extent upheld the founding characteristics of modern antropocentrism. This development of anthropocentrics can therefore be referred to as *late-modern anthropocentric environmental ethics*.[8] This form of environmental ethics characterises a great number of influential environmental reports that started to appear during the 1980s. Some examples were given in chapter two, e.g. 'Our Common Future' and 'Agenda 21', in which the term 'sustainable development' was introduced.

Late-modern anthropocentrism shares a point of departure with modern anthropocentrism, in that they both prioritise the needs and interests of humankind. Only humans have intrinsic value and the natural environment is valued partly in terms of its economic worth and partly because of the enjoyment that experiencing the natural world can give. It also shares the same optimistic opinions on economic growth and technological development. An important difference is, though, that the late-modern approach supports the goal of an enhanced quality of life, in contrast to the original goal of increased material wealth.

In the case of moral responsibilities in our interaction with nature, the matter of the fair distribution of global resources remains. The difference between the two approaches lies in the fact that the late-modern approach recognises our moral responsibilities towards future generations. An important insight which lies behind late-modern anthropocentrism is that the technical knowledge we possess can have far reaching effects on the lives of humans for hundreds or possibly thousands of years into the future, so that we should therefore develop ethical restrictions for the application of this technology. These restrictions in our interaction with the natural world would be dictated by our consideration of the future generations and not by nature itself.

A future ethic of this kind does, however, raise a number of questions. How far into the future do our responsibilities stretch; must we take two, three or ten or more of the coming generations into consideration? Does the responsibility diminish in relation to how

8   See chapter six for details about the late-modern society.

distant the generations are? Even if our responsibilities lie in our concern of the coming generations, what do we know about their needs and interests? To what extent are these assumed interests to be approached? Is it enough to ensure that they have the means to survive, or should they be able to enjoy the same quality of life as we do today; or should future generations have the opportunity to improve on that life quality?

A common opinion within this environmentally ethical approach towards these questions is that our utilization of natural resources will unavoidably affect the conditions for future generations. This is ethically acceptable since we, by means of continued technological development and use of alternative resources, can ensure that future generations have equal opportunities for a good life. Continued scientific development is, therefore, necessary in order for this ethical approach to be considered acceptable. Contrary to modern anthropocentrism's exploitation of the natural world, late-modern anthropocentrism points out that all technological development must be in accord with nature.

Problems Encountered in Anthropocentrism

From a philosophical viewpoint, anthropocentrism can be seen as problematic in that it supports the belief that humankind has a higher value than all other organisms.[9] Today's secular western world makes any reference to religious ethics to defend this position seem invalid. The claims stated by Immanuel Kant that only those capable of moral thought are morally relevant (humankind) are not unproblematic either: on what grounds can one claim that those who cannot act morally cannot therefore have intrinsic value? We cannot expect a forest to act morally towards humans, but if we feel that a forest has intrinsic value then it is logical to assume that it should also be morally relevant.

Neither is it an easy task to identify a characteristic which is unique to humankind and which gives us a moral superiority. What do we actually know about animals' souls, consciousness and sense

---

9   I.e. we have the right to appoint ourselves as evaluators, and we also have intrinsic values which distinguish us from all other forms of life.

of reason etc? If we were to find a characteristic that could be regarded as unique, who is to determine that it is just that aspect which assures moral value? There is also the risk of choosing a human characteristic simply because we are humans, since we are directly involved in the dispute as well as being both judge and jury. It is equally problematic when creating a hierarchy of values based on certain attributes. If a certain attribute allows for a higher moral value, then who is to claim otherwise if we rank humankind based on that attribute? If the capacity to reason gives humans a higher ranking than animals, it is logical to assume that those people who are more capable of reasoning will be valued higher than those who are not so gifted – a suggestion in direct conflict with our basic understanding of all humans being equal.

The following section will illustrate those environmentally ethical approaches that are based on other reference points and that have extended their moral sphere to include more than just human life.

Non-anthropocentric Environmental Ethics

Anthropocentric ethics can be said to be the main orientation of the modern age in the case of humankind's relationship with the natural world. As mentioned earlier, in chapter two, there has always been a varying degree of resistance towards this approach.[10] A prominent source of resistance was the Romantic Movement, which originated in the end of the 18th Century. The Romantics reacted strongly towards the modern age's mechanical and atomistic view of the natural world and insisted that nature was a living entity which was best likened to an organism with a soul and a will to live. Humankind was a part of this totality and estranging itself from nature was regarded as leading to moral decline.

---

10 See Worster (1994) on how the contrasting ideas of controlling the natural world or adapting to it have shared varying degrees of popularity throughout modern history.

103

In recent years, a number of more or less radical alternatives to the anthropocentric ethic have also been put forward, which in many cases have been rooted in the Romantic Movement. These opinions have always held a strong position within the alternative environmental movements, and are closely related to the type of environmental commitment we described as 'deep ecology' (see chapter two).

Most of those claiming non-anthropocentric ethical standpoints see humankind as belonging to the natural world and having an organic worldview. Additionally, humans are not considered as having an exclusive position in the field of ethical thought. As was mentioned above, the non-anthropocentric standpoints can be presented in two categories: *biocentric* ethics and *ecocentric* ethics. We will begin this study by taking a closer look at the biocentric alternative.

Biocentrism

Bios is the Greek word for 'life'; biocentric therefore means to put life in focus. Within the biocentric movement it is thought that not only humans, but other living organisms also have intrinsic or inherent worth. This belief implies that the lives of plants and animals can also be complete within themselves and therefore have moral relevance. Accordingly, we should restrict our interaction with nature, not for our own benefit but out of consideration for other living organisms.

Biocentrists believe that we do not possess any specific qualities that allow us to assume an ethically superior position in the world. There are, on the other hand, certain qualities which unify different forms of life and also give moral relevance to other life forms. The reasons that oblige humankind to take other organisms into consideration on moral grounds differ somewhat among philosophers. Some of these reasons are as follows:

- the ability to experience suffering;[11]

---

11   This is one of the founding arguments for many of philosophers who support animal rights e.g. Peter Singer (1987).

- the striving for self realisation and the fact that other organisms also strive to develop themselves to their fullest potential;[12]
- that other life forms have an inherent will to live;[13]
- that other life forms have their own interests and strive to achieve goals in order to benefit themselves.[14]

The next question is whether or not the above points apply to all organisms on planet Earth, and if so, does this then imply that all life forms are of equal value. Or, alternatively, to whom and how much consideration should humans take in our interaction with the natural world? Some biocentrists believe that all life is born with inherent worth (independent of human involvement) and these are the same conditions for all life forms. Others claim that humans should accredit all life forms with intrinsic value, and that the value is dependent on the various species' capacity to experience suffering, conscious thought and a quality of life etc. This implies a hierarchy within the species which can act as a guide in any conflict of values. Another standpoint is that the physical/mental capacities of the species are so varied that it is only those with certain features that we are morally obliged to respect. A common standpoint is, for example, that only those who can experience suffering have intrinsic value and are morally relevant.[15]

Although there are certain differences among the various representatives of biocentrism, the movement is in full agreement on the demands of the moral responsibility of humans towards the interests and needs of other life forms. This opinion has given rise to a number of extensively debated questions concerning how the conflict between the interests of humankind and the interests of animals can be dealt with e.g.:

---

12 Inspired by the 17th Century philosopher Spinoza, Arne Naess (1989) presents this argument in his ecosophical approach.
13 This thought is a main point in Albert Schweitzer's "Reverence for Life"-ethics (1998), which is based on the Christian philosophy.
14 This claim is held by Paul Taylor (1986/1989), one of the most influential representatives of biocentrism today.
15 Singer states that we do not have any ethical responsibilities towards life forms which do not experience feelings (e.g. mussels and other basic life forms), whilst on the other hand Schwietzer would probably contend that the principle of life is present in all life forms and they must therefore all be treated with respect.

- What do we have the right to eat? If we have to kill in order to survive, is it more correct to kill plants than animals?
- Is it right to have animals as pets or is this a violation of animals' rights? Do animals suffer more in captivity than they do in the wild?
- Do plants have rights? Is it, for instance, right to throw house-plants away once they start looking a bit withered?
- Should animal testing be permitted? If so, where should the line be drawn? Is it acceptable to test cosmetic products on animals, or should it just be permitted in the development of life saving pharmaceuticals?
- Is it immoral to hunt and fish unless it is necessary for survival? Since it is generally accepted that humans eat meat, is it then wrong to hunt game living freely in the natural environment, which in turn reduces the need for keeping animals on farms?

In practice a radical biocentric lifestyle would be problematical, since it would demand far-reaching changes in our current cultural climate. In particular, the conflict between human and environmental ethics creates many difficult problems – not least the fact that there is a conflict of values when we are faced with the idea that an animal's life is equal in value to a human's life, even though we have an ethical understanding that states that all life holds the same value.

Another problem is actually determining the precise interests of plants and animals; what are, for example, the interests of a squirrel or a bee? One option is to allocate an interest based on our own knowledge and apply the same intuition we would use if were we caring for a person who, for whatever reason, cannot communicate with the outside world.[16]

An important question in the tension that exists between biocentric and human ethics is the problem referred to in chapter one, namely whether humankind is primarily a biological or a cultural

---

16 We do, for instance, usually follow the will or interests of a a person who we
    believe to be dead, unconscious or suffering from some sort of impairment.

life form. Based on the first standpoint it seems reasonable that humans occupy a specific ecological niche e.g. that it is natural to kill and eat those life forms which we were created to eat and to protect ourselves from parasites and predators etc. The second standpoint implies claims which define humankind as being a cultural life form with the ability to go beyond our natural instincts, and with our cultural development make ethically based decisions e.g. choosing a different food source than our hunter gatherer ancestors.

Ecocentrism

Ecocentrism is a non-anthropocentric, environmental ethical belief which can be seen as an expansion of biocentrism, although it does have some slightly differing reference points. 'Eco' comes from the Greek *oikos*, which means house, but it also can be understood as the entity in which we all live (thus it can be understood in the same way as 'eco' in 'ecology', see chapter four). For biocentrists, only living organisms have intrinsic value or inherent worth, but for ecocentrists, even biological systems e.g. ecosystems and species have either intrinsic value or inherent worth and are morally relevant.

The reasoning behind this expansion is based on a holistic theory that life is organised in whole systems, e.g. ecosystems. In the same way that countless cells together make up a dynamic organism, numerous organisms with specific characteristics and qualities make up an ecosystem with the ability to adapt and control itself. From this viewpoint, ecocentrists believe that the ecosystems and the species therein are 'wholes' that preserve life on earth which humans, when interacting with the natural world, can either benefit or damage. Therefore we have the moral responsibility to respect and care for these biological systems when we interact with the environment.

The ecocentrists prioritise the 'whole' rather than separate units. In many ways, acting with consideration towards entire systems involves a completely different approach than that which would benefit individuals.[17] The norm is to interact in such a way that the biological systems remain intact and stable (even the word 'beautiful' is used by some ecocentrists) and that they maintain their capacity to develop and evolve in all their diversity.

But many consider the consequences of the norm that the totality is superior to the individual as quite problematic. Ecocentrism has also been accused of 'ecofascism', i.e. the freedom of individuals is subordinate to the well being of biological systems. A central question is therefore, how concerned should we be in the preservation of whole systems in relation to the interests of individuals? In particular, the concern for 'wholes' in relation to human values, needs and desires is a difficult issue.

According to ecocentrism, in matters dealing with more general questions of social development, the values associated with biological wholes should be prioritised above human interests. This opinion demands minimum negative human influence as a key element in social development plans, and that we try to achieve certain goals such as a reduction in population figures and a reduction in resource exploitation. Other achievements include preserving natural areas that up until now have been untouched by humans, in addition to restoring areas that have been damaged by human involvement.

The Conflict Between Human Ethics and Environmental Ethics

In our study of biocentrism and ecocentrism, we have encountered several problems where the principles of environmental ethics are in conflict with basic human values. It therefore seems reasonable

---

17   It is important to note here that there are differences in the consequences of the ecocentric approach compared with the biocentric (especially in the case of animal rights). According to ecocentrists, species are more important than individuals and therefore there is not the same commitment to reducing the suffering of individuals within a species. Natural suffering and natural exploitation of resources that are in agreement with our evolutionary role in the ecosystem – e.g. eating meat – is considered acceptable. It is considered equally acceptable to keep animals in captivity as long as they do not suffer more than they would in their natural environment. For biocentrists, on the other hand, it is fundamentally unacceptable to deprive a creature of its freedom.

that we take a closer look at these types of problems and suggest various ways of relating to these conflicts from a non-anthropocentric (mainly ecocentric) perspective.

The simplest reason for these conflicts is the fact that we are dealing with two separate systems of ethics: environmental ethics which concerns questions on our relationship with the natural world and all other life forms, and human ethics which involves questions of how humans live together in society. These belief systems are governed by norms that cannot easily be applied outside the contexts in which they were created. It is in the situations where these ethical principles clash that conflicts arise, and the resulting question is always which principles should prevail. It is when environmentally ethical principles are prioritised in favour of human ethical principles that one runs the risk of being labelled as an 'environmental fascist'.

This problem can be illustrated with an exercise on values which is used in teaching environmental ethics in schools and teacher training colleges. The exercise is based on the following macabre scenario: 'You are out driving along a forest road and, after turning a corner, are met by the following scene: a car with the driver and a dog have hit an elk and a wolf, which had been chasing the elk. The driver of the car, the dog, the elk and the wolf are all lying on the road in a critical condition. Being medically trained you immediately realise that not all of them will survive and you must prioritise; the first to receive your attention will have the best chance of survival. In which order would you try to save these creatures?'

Based on the strict principles of ecocentrism it would be completely acceptable to choose the wolf first, since they are an endangered species and are therefore of greatest importance to the bio diversity. For many people, however, this choice would almost certainly be in conflict with our spontaneous moral reaction that the human life is the most important. Is it ethically possible to defend this type of choice and still maintain an ecocentric perspective?

In solving this kind of problem, many ecocentric philosophers would rationalise in the following way. We must clearly take the entire bio diversity into consideration e.g. species and ecosystems, but the individuals which constitute the whole can be prioritised first. This is due to the fact that the individuals also have intrinsic value and are consequently equally important or even more important than the whole. It is also possible to give precedence to human ethics in conflicts concerning both human and environmental ethics. Humans can, for instance, be accredited with a higher intrinsic value compared with the same values of biological systems. According to this ethical standpoint, it can therefore be justifiable to chop down an untouched forest in order to ensure traffic safety, as this would result in saving human lives. Another option to take when prioritising humans is to refer to the principle that states that it is natural and acceptable to prioritise that which is closest to us: our families, people, the society we are part of etc.

To reduce the tension between the natural and cultural worlds, one can ask the question: on which level do the differing interests lie in each situation where value conflicts arise? It seems reasonable to utilise natural resources in order to satisfy basic human needs, but when this utilisation crosses the boundary from human needs to entertainment and luxury, it becomes ethically unjustifiable from a non-anthropocentric perspective. The difficult question is: who draws the line for what is considered luxury and basic requirements in today's cultural climate?

A guiding principle in environmental ethics can be that the value which an action has for humans must exceed the intrinsic values held by the organisms who suffer as a result of the act. We can, for example, ask ourselves how we should value the joy of having a bunch of wild flowers on the dining table in relationship to the loss of life involved for the flowers.

Summary

In this chapter it has been our aim to demonstrate how humans can relate to the problematic environmental situation and how this relationship can be based on values. Various authors and philosophers have developed different approaches in environmental ethics to act as guidelines in our interaction with nature. The following table illustrates the points of departure and the basic principles of the different categories of environmental ethics:

	Modern Anthropo-centrism	Late-modern Anthropo-centrism	Biocentrism	Ecocentrism
Philosophical Origins	The Enlight-enment	The Enlight-enment	The Roman-tic Move-ment	The Roman-tic Move-ment
View of Nature	Mechanical	Mechanical	Organic	Organic
Moral rele-vance	People alive today	People alive today and future generations	People and other living individuals	People, other organisms and biologi-cal wholes (species, ecosystems, landscapes)
Relationship to nature	Humankind separate from nature Natural world should be control-led and dominated	Humankind as a part of nature Natural world should be control-led and cultivated for the benefit of humans	Humankind as a part of nature Adaptation and consider-ation to other life forms	Humankind as a part of nature Adaptation to nature for the benefit of the develop-ment of all biological systems

Perhaps the most important difference lies in the successive expansion of environmental ethics: from *modern anthropocentrism* mainly restricted to human life, via *late-modern anthropocentrism* where future generations became a concern, to *biocentrism* in which other living individuals were included, and finally to *ecocentrism* which includes whole biological systems.

From the perspective of problematic environmental issues as value questions, there are no objective solutions or absolute 'rights' or 'wrongs'. There are no scientific answers to the question of to what degree and in what way we have the right to exploit the natural world for the well being of humans. Within the different approaches to environmental ethics, different debates have developed which address how we should relate to the natural world and the living organisms therein. As we have seen, all these approaches present both advantages and disadvantages.

Applying these approaches in morally correct interaction with the natural world has also proved to be a difficult process. A strict adoption of certain environmental ethics often results in many practical problems in peoples' daily lives. One possible solution can be to make moral judgements in relation to the specific circumstances of each individual case and by applying principles of environmental ethics to guide us in evaluating the outcomes of our interaction with nature.

Another aspect that can cause difficulties in moral correctness when dealing with the environment is the fact that it is often not possible to directly experience the consequences of our actions, since the results will not be apparent until some time in the future. This can be compared with our interaction with other people in daily life where we often receive a direct response to our actions. We can evaluate the consequences of our interaction with people and we also experience satisfaction if we have benefited people in some way. The consequences of moral actions in an environmental situation are often very difficult to detect or only possible to see at some time in the distant future. Here our actions are very small parts of a complete network of human action. This makes it much harder to experience an 'environmentally moral intuition' compared with the moral intuition in interaction with other human beings.

In teaching, this presents a great challenge in creating opportunities for school pupils to develop a conscious approach to environmental ethics as well as developing sensitivity in their approach to environmental moral issues and dilemmas.

Further Reading

The following books are recommended for further reading about the topics of environmental ethics:

Callicott, J. Baird (1989). *In Defence of the Land Ethics: Essays in Environmental Philosophy.* New York: SUNY Press.

Callicott, J. Baird (1999). *Beyond the Land Ethics: More Essays in Environmental Philosophy.* New York: SUNY Press.

Norton, Bryan G. (1987). *Why Preserve Natural Variety?* Princeton: Princeton University Press.

Des Jardins, Joseph (1997). *Environmental Ethics: An Introduction to Environmental Philosophy.* Belmont: Wadsworth Publishing Company.

Van DeVeer, Donald & Pierce, Christine (Eds.) (1998). *The Environmental Ethics and Policy Book: Philosophy, Ecology, Economics.* Belmont: Wadsworth Publishing Company.

Zimmerman, Michael E. (Ed.) (1993). *Environmental Philosophy: From Animal Rights to Radical Ecology.* Englewood Cliffs New Jersey: Prentice Hall.

Other Reference Literature

Merchant, Carolyn (1980). *The Death of Nature: Women, Ecology, and the Scientific Revolution.* San Francisco: Harper & Row.

Naess, Arne (1989). *Ecology, Community and Lifestyle: Outline of an Ecosophy* (translated and revised by David Rothenburg). Cambridge: Cambridge University Press.

Singer, Peter (Ed.) (1987). *In Defence of Animals.* New York: Blackwell Publishers Ltd.

Schweitzer, Albert (1998). *Out of My Life and Thought: An Autobiography.* Baltimore: John Hopkins U.P.

Taylor, Paul W. (1986/1989). *Respect for Nature: A Theory of Environmental Ethics.* Princeton: Princeton.

Worster, Donald (1994). *Nature's Economy: A History of Ecological Ideas.* Cambridge: Cambridge University Press.

6 Environmental Problems from a Political Point of View

In the previous chapter we presented some of the different ways of seeing humankind's relationship with nature, as well as alternative suggestions as to how humankind should interact with nature. In society, it is necessary to organise all these different standpoints, interests and demands in the form of collective agreements, which are then implemented to ensure that society and the natural environment remain in a preferred balance, deal with environmental problems and decide how natural resources are to be shared etc.

In managing the societal aspect of environmental problems, we must be able to relate current environmental issues to today's society. We need theories that can help us understand the various transformations which society has been through, the conditions for social life existing in today's society and the changes that are currently taking place.

In the field of social sciences during recent decades, there has been a great deal of debate on the state of social and cultural climates within western societies. One aspect that many of the changes have in common is that they challenge, in various ways, the founding ideas, lifestyles and structures of modern industrial society.

Theories on the transformations within society have had a great deal of influence in social science debates. A number of specialists – mainly sociologists – have formulated certain ideas which have had great impact on the way research into environmental issues is carried out in today's society. The main focus in this chapter will be the debate within the social sciences on the changing role of science, and how this change allows us to see environmental issues from a *political perspective.*

The current perspectives also put questions on the aims and purposes of environmental education under scrutiny. This implies that there is good reason to look more closely at these theories in respect to our study on how to address environmental and developmental issues in schools.

We will introduce the chapter with a more detailed description of those ideas previously mentioned in the book, which are usually associated with the *modern project*. These ideas can be said to represent the development of the modern industrialised society and the strong position held by scientific study and research. This will be followed by a presentation of the opinions of leading sociologists on the definitions of today's *late-modern* society and the present environmental situation, which they claim is a consequence of the modern project. Additionally, there will be a theoretical *post-modern* critique of the modern approach and the highly influential role of the scientific community. Finally, conclusions will be drawn from the late-modern and post-modern perspectives as to the *political* character of the whole environmental issue.

The Modern Project

The modern age is said to have its origins in the scientific revolution at the beginning of the 17th Century (see chapter one). However, it is mainly during the Age of Enlightenment in the 18th Century that modern thought began to be developed and cultivated. As a result of the Enlightenment, the modern approach received attention as a philosophical project, i.e. that definite objectives were associated with this new way of reasoning. The Enlightenment was characterised by a belief that humans were independent beings who were rational by nature and acted with their own and their fellow beings' best interests in mind. The modern project was concerned with liberating this potential from authorities and dogmatic systems of thought (mainly religious) which had, since the Middle Ages, controlled the worldview of most people. The philosophers of the Enlightenment claimed that each person should make decisions and choices in life by applying reason and common sense. A motto of the Enlightenment was 'Always think for yourself'.

The Search for Universal Truths and Goodness

The thinkers of the Enlightenment believed that free individuals must have access to objective facts in order to form an independent understanding of important issues. It is the duty of the scientific community to supply people with these facts. The natural world is seen as being governed by laws, which are mechanical, constant and logical; consequently it is possible for human reason to understand them. The task of the natural sciences is to find the correct method to investigate the natural world so that a true definition of it can be presented. Ideally, scientific truths should be completely free of any subjective evaluations.

However, not only knowledge but also correct value judgements are considered logical and universal. This implies that the studies of philosophy and humanities can pin down definite and objective answers to any ethical and political questions, which arise in the same way that the natural sciences present definite and objective answers to questions concerning the natural world.

In order to supply objective answers to questions on truth and goodness, it is seen as necessary to establish a strong neutral ground that can serve as a reference point for all human thought and action. The search for this point of reference is based on the belief that there is a reality regardless of *whether* it is experienced or *how* it is experienced. This viewpoint is usually referred to as *realism*.

Therefore, the modern philosophical and scientific goal can be said to be based on the attempt to create a definite reference point on which a universal theory can be formed, i.e. a theory on truth and goodness which is valid for all time and completely independent of individual interests and desires. A theory of this kind would apply to every branch of science.

A main point in the modern project is that humans, with the help of science, can exert *control* over their lives. Above all it is the idea that, with the knowledge of the laws of nature, one is able to govern natural processes and adapt the natural world according to human desires.[1] By applying science and technology, humankind

---

1 This could be compared with the definition of nature given in chapter one: the natural world makes up the elements and processes which humans do not consciously control. Based on this definition it can be said that one of the aims of the the modern project is to conquer the natural world and transform nature to culture (from 'wilderness' to cultural landscape).

will thus move towards a better future. Through an increasingly more effective exploitation of natural resources, material standards in society will improve as will the welfare of people. Science is, in this way, a method of controlling the development of society. Science and reason can also be applied to control people themselves. By means of education and the development of reason, people become cultivated and their primitive urges and instincts are restrained. With the help of science humans become liberated, not only from secular and religious authorities, but also from the forces of nature. The purpose of the so-called 'grand narrative' of the modern project can therefore be explained as liberating people by allowing them access to a scientifically based education.

The modern project is thus strongly associated with the belief of reason and science, and also the belief that a tangible, objective point of reference that can be applied when defining nature and social life is necessary to avoid social chaos and moral decline.

The Late-modern Society

But where have the modern project, science and reason led us? A number of leading sociologists, such as Ulrich Beck and Anthony Giddens[2], claim that in today's cultural environment we exist in something which is described as a late-modern state of being and that we live in a late-modern society. In spite of society having undergone a number of radical transformations, it is implied that it is still following the path of development that was started in the modern project. This means, among other things, that science and reason continue to have a leading role in late-modern societies. How, then, will late-modern thinkers characterise contemporary society?

---

2   See Beck (1992) and Giddens (1991). Even if there are many differences between the two, there are similarities in their ways of dealing with the matters in question here. They will be referred to in this text as 'the late-modern sociologists'.

The Reflexive Society

A central term in the late-modern theory on our present situation is *reflexivity:* this means that human beings possess the property of self-consciousness – they are able to reflect on themselves, their situations and relationships. Through the liberation from authority and our understanding of reason, which was a result of the modern project, we now have the capability of questioning our own abilities and opportunities. This also applies to life on a social level, and we can therefore speak in terms of late-modernity as being a reflexive modernity.[3] We can, in turn, also question the reference points and goals we have in the development of society. In this late-modern state of existence, the development of society cannot be said to have any given goals; these goals are constantly under deliberation and negotiation and therefore constantly in a state of change.

Abandoning Traditions

Throughout history, traditions have been highly influential guidelines and have prescribed both small and large aspects of humans' lives. This applied to opinions and values as it did much as to free time activities and vocational choices. These traditions could have been connected to the close family and relations, local communities, social class, ethnicity, gender etc. Traditions have, to a great extent, imposed limitations on humans' lives, but they also afforded security to individuals, families and communities.

Reflexivity has made it possible for us to question traditional ways of living. There seems to be a tendency to display an ever-increasing abandonment of values, norms and institutions associated with traditions. 'It's always been done this way' is no longer a valid argument in today's society. Freed from traditions, we are faced with a number of options on how we are to live our lives.

In a multicultural and pluralistic society we encounter a diversity of life styles. There are many variations of 'family life' and the choice of profession is no longer determined by social background.

3   This term is used by both Beck and Giddens.

Moreover, there is a multitude of sub-cultures with varying life styles to choose from. When group or social affiliations have less and less significance, the society is said to become *individualistic;* individuals are to take responsibility for their own lives and create their own life projects. However, at the same time, many people seek security in authorities and strong public figures that receive a lot of attention in the mainstream media. From these two opposing points we can see a contrast in the loss of traditions; we have gained freedom but lost security.

A Changing Identity

From the late-modern perspective, our identity is seen as being socially and culturally dependent. Initially this means that our identity is in a *perpetual state of change.* Secondly, it implies that we as individuals can possess *a number of identities* depending on the situation and context in which we are acting. This could explain why, in certain situations, we have difficulties in living up to values we feel committed to in other situations (imagine, for instance, a student who strongly advocates a radical ecocentric environmental ethical standpoint in environmental discussions in school; but in his/her free time travels hundreds of kilometres to go skiing on artificial snow at a resort in, until very recently, untouched mountain landscapes).

Ambivalence Towards Science

Reflexivity has also resulted in our relationship with science becoming characterised by a degree of ambivalence. Science and technology have, of course, asserted a certain amount of control over the natural world; enough to remove the direct dependency on the forces of nature, which in turn has afforded us a comfortable lifestyle. This has resulted in a dependency relationship with technology and science. We need scientific and technical experts so we can both understand and function in our daily lives. We use equipment e.g. computers, cars or electric tooth brushes, without actually knowing how they actually work or how to repair them if they break down. One example is the fact that there are cars being produced where the bonnet can only be opened at authorised garages. We live in a complex, abstract, high technological and globalised society in which it is possible to only understand a small part of. We are involved daily in a large number of abstract systems: economic, energy, food supply, information, politics etc.

Science has not managed to supply the definite answers that the philosophers of the Enlightenment had hoped for. There is still a lot of disagreement surrounding many questions and the scientific theories are also constantly being revised and rewritten. This has resulted in doubts as to whether science actually has the potential to endow humankind with a good life and a good society.

The Risk Society

The uncertainty of the capabilities and limitations of the scientific world are perhaps most clearly visible in connection with environmental issues. The late-modern social theorists are among the first to have seriously integrated environmental issues into understanding society.[4] Central to these theories is the term *risk*. This term was mainly associated with the sociologist Ulrich Beck who introduced the term *risk society* in the 1980s.[5]

The risk society is a state in the development of western societies characterised by a global economy based on far reaching scientific and technological development.[6] According to Beck, such a society is in a position to allow people a good social and material standard of living, although there is also a certain amount of risk or *hazard* involved in such a practice. These hazards are part of the social

---

4 It can be also noted that the German sociologists Theodor Adorno and Max Horkheimer sharply criticised humankind's attempted dominance of the natural world as early as the 1940's in "Dialectic of Enlightenment" (1969).

5 The term was introduced by Beck in the book Risk Society: *Towards a New Modernity* (1992; In German: *Risikogesellschaft: Auf dem Weg in eine andere Moderne*, published in 1986) and received a great deal of attention. The term is also used by Giddens.

6 The risk society is a development of industrialised society. These types of society can be considered theoretical ideals. Therefore we cannot actually claim that we are living in a risk society, but might be heading towards one – the term indicates an orientation.

structure and therefore there is nothing we can do about them as long as the present social climate prevails. Prosperity and hazards develop together, so to speak hand in hand. The hazards are associated with the development of technological systems; energy systems create hazards such as nuclear reactor meltdowns, the transportation system creates hazards which affect the climate, chemical usage creates hazards by poisoning natural habitats etc. We do not know in advance what the result of technological development will be, e.g. nobody could predict the thinning of the ozone layer, and nobody can be sure of when or where the next nuclear power station meltdown will take place. This is why it seems more appropriate to discuss hazards rather than risks – a risk is something that we consciously take and can calculate, whereas hazards are more unpredictable and extremely difficult to control effectively.

Characterising Environmental Problems

According to late-modern sociologists, what is it that specifically characterises the environmental hazards in today's risk society? Humans have always been exposed to all kinds of hazards. The difference, however, is that earlier in history these hazards came from outside the sphere of influence of societies e.g. earthquakes, crop failure, and epidemics. Humans themselves *unintentionally manufacture* the hazards in risk societies. They are the consequences of our actions, although we have not consciously chosen the hazards which we created, e.g. when the western nations chose to develop energy networks powered by fossil fuels, such aspects as acid rain and greenhouse gases were not included in the planning but were an unavoidable consequence of it.

One of the most defining characteristics of modern society is the unprecedented *pace of development*. Additionally, there is also an intensive interaction between local and global activities. Our daily lives are influenced by and dependent on events that take place in distant locations all over the world, as well as our own activities also having global implications. This results in hazards becoming both more diffuse and abstract and increasingly difficult for 'normal' people to understand and relate to.

The environmental problems of today can be said to have moved the boundaries of both *space and time.* For example, it is impossible to predict where and when the greenhouse effect will manifest itself, as it is a constant process that has been in effect for a long time and will continue for many years into the future. We all contribute to this problem on a varying scale and on a daily basis, and people, animals and plants all over the world are more or less affected. In this way, environmental issues even eradicate *national and class boundaries.* Even if developing countries and poor people are generally more exposed to the effects of environmental problems, it is only a matter of time before the privileged will also begin suffering from the effects of environmental damage. In the long term it would be in everybody's interest to deal with environmental problems in the most effective ways possible.

The Possibilities of Environmental Commitment from the Late-modern Perspective

What is, then, the best way of dealing with a situation known for its conflicts and hazards? The late-modern sociologists continue to have faith in the potential of the modern project, although there are areas of disagreement. Giddens claims that it is important to remain aware of the limitations of the modern project, and he refers to the hazards created by technological development as an example. Additionally, he states that whereas science and reason can supply answers to questions on the actual make up of the world, they are of no benefit in existential matters and questions of values e.g. that which constitutes a good life.

When addressing the issue of environmental commitment, both Beck and Giddens seem to agree on the importance of grounding this commitment on a solid base. In this sense they are confident that both reason and the scientific community are capable of forming the basis for democratic solutions to environmental problems.

As stated earlier, late-modern thinkers have stressed that we have created a social situation in which we can no longer monitor the consequences of our actions. Since we can only physically detect a small number of hazards, we have become dependent on scientific resources to discover these hazards for us. Even though scientists are not always in complete agreement, their collective knowledge constitutes a basis from which we can understand the world and the changing environment. If there were no scientific research into the changes in the biosphere, it is likely that we would still be ignorant of the greenhouse effect, the thinning of the ozone layer, the depletion of species or acidification. The acceptance of scientific definitions of environmental problems is also a standard requirement if they are to be addressed in the public debate.

Very few people, however, have access to scientific reports on environmental issues. Most of us receive information about environmental threats and damage through mainstream media sources. This implies that how the media depicts environmental issues has a great effect on the collective awareness of the general public. Independent media sources are therefore essential in democratic debates on environmental issues.

Both Beck and Giddens have a great deal of faith in human reason and our ability to deal democratically with environmental issues in a morally correct way. According to Beck, the solutions to problems lies within our ability to reflect on our self and our present situation. With a continued liberation of reason we can achieve progress by maintaining a healthy criticism of the lifestyles and societies we have created. It is also through reason that we can increase our awareness of the fact that environmental issues are a global concern which we all share. In this way Beck hopes to uproot the traditional beliefs in 'us and them', 'now and later', and 'here and there', and in doing so form a feeling of solidarity which spans across space and time as well as the divisions of classes within society.

Post-modern Challenges

The theories on late-modern society discussed above can be seen as a description of what it is like to live in contemporary society from a certain perspective. Parallel with these theories, a number of social scientists have appeared who have either referred to themselves or have been classified as *post-modern*. The word *post* in post-

124

modern implies that it describes something which follows modernity. Post-modern theories are, however, not descriptions of a period in society but rather a theoretical perspective – a way of thinking or relating to life and society.

If the late-modern theories can be seen as a critical development of modernity, then the post-modern approach represents a comprehensive critique of the ideas of modernity, where even the late-modern ideas are questioned. The main criticism is aimed at one of the founding ideas in modern thought i.e. the belief that it is possible to form a system of knowledge that is valid for all cultures for all time.

Disputing Universal Truths and Goodness

The post-modern theorists[7] dispute any claims that there might be a possibility of discovering a universal truth or something which is universally 'good'. They mean that in spite of the exhaustive efforts of science and philosophy, the attempts to find anything that is not dependent on a particular culture have failed.

The post-modernists claim that it is simply not possible to define a constant, neutral basis from which we can objectively relate to the world and our lives. This is why it has never been possible to formulate an all-encompassing theory which can combine and unite the numerous branches of science and philosophy.

As a result, both science and philosophy have been divided into various disciplines and orientations, where each division has developed its respective methods and criteria for determining what is true or right and good. Instead of a 'grand narrative' about the truths of the world and how we should live 'the good life' and create 'the good society', there are a great many 'local narratives' about what is true, good, and right. In light of this we can speak in terms of a diversity of understandings and explanations. Another keyword in this area is *contingency,* which can be said to represent the idea that the development of things is not predetermined and

---

7   This section is based on the works of the authors: Jean-François Lyotard (1997); Stanley Aronwitz, & Henry Giroux, (1997); Robin Usher & Richard Edwards (1996) and Gert Biesta (1998).

therefore to a lesser degree predictable. The post-modernists agree that the states of pluralism and contingency should be considered as positive. With a larger range of options, they feel that there are increased opportunities for making the correct choices with regard to our own lives and the future development of society.

In post-modern thought, no knowledge can be said to be independent of the contexts, reasons and fields of interest from which it came. In claiming that a source of knowledge is absolute and universally applicable, one would automatically be restricting and censoring other sources of knowledge. This is why a certain amount of criticism is aimed at the highly influential and exclusive position of science in today's society. By questioning universal theories, doors to other perspectives and definitions on life are opened, which means that we can perceive the world in ways other than those of the traditional sciences. For example, one can ask if the knowledge held by botanical research on rainforests is more valid and reliable than the tradition and experienced-based knowledge of the indigenous populations who actually live in the forests? In post-modern thought, the idea that reason is the only path to knowledge is also disputed, and here it is understood that emotions and aesthetics are also important aspects of fully understanding the world and ourselves.

The post-modernists hold that the faith in the 'grand narrative' of modernity, and the possibilities of reaching a good life through science and reason, has lost its power. They mean that there are tendencies in society which suggest that people have begun to doubt science and its advocates, and are looking to alternative sources for answers pertaining to life and the nature of things. One example is the popularity of New Age Movement; another is that many people turn to alternative health care methods rather than relying on traditional western medicine. Some people think this indicates that we are living in, or at least heading towards, a post-modern society.

Post-modern writers have also highlighted that there is a close relationship between truth and power. As we have already discussed, the modern approach was to keep the currents of scientific, objective truth and the subjective, value based political power quite separate. However, from the post-modern perspective, the truth is something that we create and not something we discover. The possession of power allows for the formulation of truths, and truths are instrumental in establishing power.

A Post-modern Perspective on Environmental Problems

According to modern thought, environmental problems are something that we *discover*. They are phenomena which take place in reality and which can be described in words i.e. as they actually are. With an appropriate description, then, we can analyse, calculate and predict risks. In modern thought, the task of science is to supply the general public with objective information on environmental problems around the world, which will, among other things, help people to make political decisions.

From a post-modern perspective, what we consider as environmental problems are related to the way we perceive the world. We interpret and perceive the world based on the cultural settings and values with which we are surrounded. The various characteristics of the language we speak are intimately connected to the way we act and relate to the world. For example, we distinguish between humans *and* animals: the human species is special; it has its own category and is separate from all other species, which are simply known as animals. This differentiation of language can be seen as a reflection of humankind's relationship towards nature.

It is not possible 'to extract' oneself from one's own culture. Knowledge is always the result of perceiving and considering the world from certain prescribed reference points. When a system of knowledge becomes 'true', it is because a group of people who share a common perspective see this knowledge as being beneficial to, and in agreement with, their own methods of perceiving the world. It is in this way that truths and knowledge are created; they are simply based on the human activity of communicating our perspectives, the results of our enquiries and observations.[8] Knowledge can be seen as a social agreement based on our experiences of the world which make a common understanding of the world possible.

---

8   The social theorist Niklas Luhman (1989) states that the reason why environmental problems receive so little attention in social debates is that we do not communicate with the natural environment. It is only when we communicate with each other that we become aware of the threats we impose on nature. Environmental problems must then be translated into a language which is understood in society e.g. economics.

Even science has its specific points of departure, standpoints and reasons in its perception and study of the world. These aspects can be quite different between the various branches of science; there can even be variations of standpoints and values within each science.[9] This clearly implies that the scientific world cannot be neutral; all interpretations of the world are based on certain perspectives, reasons and opinions.[10] From the post-modern perspective, scientific research does not represent the only or 'true' method of perceiving the world, but represents just *one* among many perspectives. The reference points which we apply when we interpret the world are not at all similar for all people, in all cultures or at all times. When we support various standpoints within the environmental debate, they all have their reference points in different opinions, perspectives and desired achievements.

The Possibilities of Environmental Commitment from a Post-modern Perspective

One question which receives a great deal of attention, is whether or not the post-modern perspective will create a relativism which will lead to all systems of knowledge and values being regarded as equally true and good. If this happened it would result in a lack of commitment, moral decline and general chaos. If all things are equal in quality, how would it be possible to be committed to a specific cause? Here it is important to distinguish between the late-modern and post-modern perspectives. In the former, the adherence to reason and science leads towards forming a commitment to the environment and an environmental policy. In post-modernism, however, pluralism is the key word in environmental commitment and policy formation. This is because every decision concerning commitment and policy will always lead to certain standpoints, values and information having precedence, whilst

---

9   Worster (1994) claims that within ecology there are different standpoints of values that have influenced how people have described the development and function of nature.

10 An example is the modern natural sciences concern with exerting control over the natural world, based on a value-based position on the rights of human to exploit nature.

others are rejected. Therefore, there is a striving among many post-modernists, to bring the lesser known opinions to the fore, and in this way increase the democratic potential within social debates.

For this reason it is important to emphasise that there is no single standpoint from which an interpretation of environmental problems can be regarded as being more correct or valid than any other. Additionally, contrasting groups in society have, with different reference points, developed their own areas of knowledge and interpretations of environmental problems. Based on these differing opinions there will be developments in our present and future environments which will be determined as being hazardous enough for steps to be taken, while others will be regarded as hazards that are acceptable enough to live with in the given circumstances. The post-modern perspective involves the acceptance of a multitude of standpoints in environmental issues, and that these issues must be understood and approached in relation to the contexts in which they appear.

Those who support the views of the post-modern approach claim that the disputation of universal truths and values does not automatically imply that a commitment to environmental issues is made more difficult. On the contrary, they suggest that this standpoint allows for more people – even minorities – becoming engaged in discussions and decision-making processes that affect the environment. Neither does this perspective imply that environmental issues become less tangible, although it does imply that we can only understand and become aware of them through our respective cultures and languages.

Any commitment to environmental issues based on the post-modern approach cannot be corroborated with any references to universal truths. Instead, the preferred post-modernist approach is that different points of view, opinions and arguments are expressed in open debates and discussions. In some cases agreements and understandings can be reached, while in other cases the opposing parties must simply attempt to accept or respect their respective differences. The norms established in processes of this kind have strong ties with a specific social and cultural context. It is also of great importance to remain aware of the fact that all these social agreements are temporary and can be disregarded if found to be invalid or unnecessary. The central guideline in this process should be that every decision is followed up with an in-depth discussion based on the knowledge that all agreements and decisions imply an exclusion of other opinions and information.

Conclusion: Environmental Problems are Political Problems

Despite a number of crucial differences of opinion, both the late-modern and post-modern perspectives allow for environmental problems to be seen in terms of *political* issues.[11] The basis for this political perspective is summarised below:

- Environmental hazards are the results of collective decisions. It is, therefore, not possible to isolate certain individuals as being responsible – we are collectively responsible for our actions.
- Science cannot speak in terms of absolutes with regard to the problems we have created; just as it can't give us a scientific answer to the question of which environmental hazards are acceptable to live with.
- Environmental hazards can be seen as a transformation which is a result of our exploitation of the natural world, which in turn create conflicts between different values and interests in areas where different people do not share the same opinion and interests.
- There are a vast number of different approaches to environmental ethics and humankind's relationship to the natural world and how we should interact with it.

On the whole this implies that we find ourselves in a situation where we share a common responsibility, but in which people generally do not share the same viewpoints and understandings, so that no obvious measures that can be taken.

---

11 The distinguishing feature in the perspectives is the understanding of that which represents the opportunities for commitment; the late-modernists prioritise reason and science, whereas pluralism is the main emphasis in the post-modern approach.

130

However, the issue still remains that our interpretations and evaluations of environmental situations, as well as our ways of dealing with them, are of vital importance to the future development of society. It is simply a matter of what kind of future society we would like to create and ultimately what opportunities and limitations people will be faced with when forming their lives. In other words: environmental issues are to the greatest extent political issues. If one pays attention to the extent that pluralism features in these issues, the democratic aspects of environmental problems become apparent. A necessary ingredient in any democracy is that we can openly discuss the various ways of understanding and relating to issues; in this case to environmental problems. Therefore, environmental politics does not only appear in the traditional political arenas (local councils and parliaments), but is constantly present in our daily lives.

The important question is how we can, in the most effective way possible, reach collective agreements from the diversity of opinions that are present in environmentally related issues. Not least in education, there is the important question of how to develop democratic attitudes as well as a level of understanding that will allow for an active participation in environmental and developmental debates in the younger generation. This question will be addressed in Part III.

Further Reading

The following books are recommended in further studies on environmental and developmental issues from a sociological point of view:

Beck, Ulrich (1992). *Risk Society: Towards a New Modernity.* London: Sage.

Giddens, Anthony (1991). *Consequences of Modernity.* Cambridge: Polity Press.

Hannigan, John A. (1995). *Environmental Sociology. A Social Constructionist Perspective.* London: Routledge.

Irwin, Alan (1995). *Citizen Science: A study of people, expertise and sustainable development.* London: Routledge.

Lash, Scott; Szerszynski, Bronislaw & Wynne, Brian (1996). *Risk, Environment and Modernity: Towards a New Ecology.* London: Sage.

Martell, Steve (1994). *Ecology and Society: An Introduction*. Cambridge: Polity Press.

Macnaghten, P. & Urry, J. (1998). *Contested Natures*. London: Sage.

Scott, William & Gough, Stephen (2004). *Key Issues in Sustainable Development and Learning: a critical review* (Chapter 1: *Framing the Issues: Complexity, Uncertainty, Risk and Necessity*). London & New York, Routledge-Falmer.

Yearley, Steven (1996). *Sociology, Environmentalism, Globalization. Reinventing the Globe*. London: Sage.

Other Reference Literature

Adorno, Theodor & Horkheimer, Max (1969). *Dialectic of Enlightenment*. New York: Seabury Press.

Aronowitz, Stanley & Giroux, Henry. (1997). *Postmodern Education: Politics, Culture & Social Criticism*. Minneapolis: University of Minnesota Press.

Biesta, Gert (1998). Postmodernism and the Repolicization of Education. *Interchance*, Vol. 26, No. 2, pp. 161–183.

Luhman, Niklas (1989). *Ecological Communication*. Cambridge: Polity press.

Lyotard, Jean-François (1997). *The Postmodern Condition: A report on Knowledge*. Manchester: Manchester University Press.

Usher, Robin & Edwards, Richard (1996). *Postmodernism and Education*. London: Routledge.

Worster, Donald (1994). *Nature's Economy: A History of Ecological Ideas*. Cambridge: Cambridge University Press.

7 Environmental Problems from an Economic Point of View

Economics and Environmental Economics

In chapter three, the concept 'market solutions' was introduced and briefly described as being a way of dealing with environmental problems increasingly preferred by industrial nations. It was initially presented as a way of making environmentally friendly products and services cheaper in relation to products and services that are harmful to the environment. This approach would allow for a more environmentally friendly society without the need for excessive and detailed regulations on when and how this is to be implemented. As the main topic of this chapter, this can be seen as part of what is often referred to as 'environmental economics'. The environmental economics approach is related to neoclassical economics and is characterised by its specific interests in prizing the environment and internalising so called 'external effects' to reduce negative environmental impact and guide the choice of resources used.

Other economic perspectives which have an effect on environmental and natural resource issues are: (i) 'resource economics', which is also a part of neoclassical economics but has closer links to how the economic aspects of e.g. agriculture and forestry can be managed as effectively as possible; and (ii) 'ecological economics', which can be seen as a broad scientific approach to society's relationship with the natural environment (similar to human ecology or environmental science) even though the economic aspects here are clearly an important element; or (iii) 'institutional economics', which can be considered as an alternative to the dominating neoclassical economical approach, but also has aspects that indicate an interest in environmental and natural resource issues.

It is also important to point out that, in addition to those concerning economics, many other perspectives could be presented as an illustration of how society is attempting to put into practice the discussions on ecology, ethics and politics which appeared in the previous chapter. Examples of other possible chapters could be social and physical planning, civil law, or international politics. A contributing factor that led to our choice of focusing on economic aspects is that economic sustainability is often specifically mentioned as an important criterion of sustainable development (along with ecological and social sustainability), even though it is frequently associated with 'resource economics' (see above) and maintaining the supply of resources. Another reason for choosing economics, and in particular environmental economics, is that it is a very popular topic in social debates and is often presented as the correct approach to achieving a sustainable society – or rather the only perspective and practical approach that is required in the matter of solving environmental problems. An additional fact is that the advocates of neoclassical economics often claim to already be in possession of all the necessary facts and information in order to understand and remedy most social issues.

For these reasons we will take a closer look at the approach of employing economics as a framework for sustainable development, and in particular focus on environmental economics as a strategy for guiding social development towards more sustainable goals. However, we will begin with some examples of the reccurring discussions that address the alternative of recognizing the conventional and dominating economic worldview as the main reason why modern development does not appear to be particularly sustainable. This will be continued by a number of points highlighting environmental economics as both suitable and sufficient for establishing policies for sustainable development. A section on opposing opinions and criticisms of this approach follows this and the chapter concludes with a general summary of economics and sustainable development.[1]

---

1   Work on this chapter has benefited greatly from many introductory readings in Swedish on the subject of environmental economics e.g. Hahn (1999); Fredman (1997) and the chapters by Markus Larsson and by Eva Friman respectively, in the book *Hela världen* (The whole world) (2003).

Economics as a Reason for Environmental Problems

Why begin a chapter on environmental economics with a section on how it is argued that economics contributes to and is a cause of many environmental problems? The reason is that the opinion that traditional (neoclassic) economic thought exclusively focuses on large scale unlimited material growth, on unregulated competition, and on free global markets and transportation is widespread – i.e. a development perspective that, according to chapter one, often damages the environment and is a typical depiction of modern industrial societies. The approach that focuses on values that are not exclusively material opposes this development perspective, and instead places the emphasis on smaller scale operations, confidence in local communities and self support (cf. sections on 'Critical Alternatives' and 'Sustainable Development' in chapter two). A classical depiction of this kind of critical perspective on economics is Ernst Friedrich Schumacher's book from 1973 with the apt title, 'Small is Beautiful: A Study of Economics as if People Mattered'. Here there is a call for what he describes as a 'Buddhist' economy, with moderation in material wealth, cooperation, shared ownership and humane technology – in contrast to continued large scale industrialization, overproduction, urbanization and unnecessary competition.[2]

A noteworthy illustration of this reccurring environmental critique of the outlook on development in economics is how the increase in gross national product (GNP increase) is often used as a universal measurement of success. A country's GNP gives no information other than the financial results of its sales of products and

---

[2] Another example of this type of division between different types of development, where one is associated with traditional economic thought *and* with environmental and natural resource destruction, is the Norwegian philosopher and author Sigmund Kvaløy (e.g. 1987). He describes the former development strategy as a 'complicated industrial growth society' and its environmentally friendly opposite is described as a 'complex life necessities society'. See also e.g. Friman (2002) for more on this discussion.

services.[3] This can mean that the GNP of a country can rise, for example, due to an increase in road traffic accidents (expensive car repairs, growth in the automobile industry and increased health care expenditure). In contrast, however, a GNP increase can also be attributed to investments in developing environmentally friendly modes of transportation (research, production of hybrid vehicles and investments in improving public transport etc.). It should be noted though, that an increase in a country's GNP gives no information about the increase in the use of material resources (energy, minerals etc.). Since it is solely a method of gauging the value of all products and services, a GNP increase can depend on e.g. that a specific service such as health care is valued more highly than in previous years. In the development of industrial societies, however, there has been a consistent relationship between GNP increases and increases in material consumption.[4]

How reasonable is it, then, to suggest that the traditional economic principles of industrial societies are largely to blame for the environmental problems that face modern society? This is of course a question that cannot easily be answered, although we can state the following:

- economic growth in material terms, including its associations with urbanization, competition, large scale production and transport networks, is just as much a central element of traditional economic thought as it is a central element in contemporary problems surrounding environmental and natural resource issues;[5]

---

3 The gross national product represents the total value of all goods and services produced in a country in one year and its increase is the increase of this total value from one year to another, in percent.
4 It should be observed that a GNP increase of a few percent in a country which already has a high GNP involves a much greater actual increase compared with a country that calculates its increase based upon a much lower GNP. It is equally important to remember that only the 'visible' products and services are included in the GNP figures (this does include public sector services, but only the production costs). A result of this is that voluntary and none-profit work is not included in GNP calculations. Consequently a country's GNP can increase as a result of a service becoming a profession e.g. childminding, which therefore qualifies the service as a contributor towards GNP figures.
5 See e.g. Friman (2002).

- additionally, as was described in chapter one, the relationship between humans and their natural surroundings has been the subject of many problems which date back to long before the economic theories of industrialised societies came to have a dominating role in social development (although the scale and speed of human induced environmental degradation has seriously increased in conjunction with our modern way of life);
- the development of classical economic theory with roots in the 18th Century stated that there was a certain ethical frame of reference in all human interactions, which included e.g. legislative procedures and the right of ownership (principles considered superior to short-term profits and losses) and it can be said with some authority that it is these rules – the economic game plan, so to speak – which have fallen short of including human-ecological aspects;
- 'common resources', such as the air and oceans, and 'external effects', such as environmentally damaging emissions, have been problem areas which neoclassical economics has consistently had great difficulties in defining and handling in a long term perspective.

Economics as an Environmental Opportunity

The central aim of environmental economics is to put the correct 'price tag' on the environment. For example, if industrial emissions pollute the air, the polluting organisation should be made to pay whatever society considers reasonable in relation to the seriousness of the damage. Equally, the variation in prices on raw materials used by industries should reflect the environmental value or problem that the respective materials represent, e.g. timber taken from shrinking rainforests or timber which has been grown for the specific purpose of paper production (under correct environmental conditions). Here we should note that:

- most of the products and services which we consume in our daily lives always involve differing costs for the environment e.g.

extracting raw materials, emissions, refuse management etc. (cf. chapter three, producing environmentally friendly bananas) as well as;

• the price of a product or service is always established in one way or the other; and perhaps this pricing is also determined by taking democratic factors and environmental consequences into consideration – a main point on the agenda of environmental economics is that environmental values should be central in deciding the prices of products and services.

An important milestone in the recent history of attempting to put the correct price on environmental resources and environmental problems is represented by the repercussions of the large oil spill from the tanker Exxon Valdez in 1989, in Alaska. In this case, the guidelines of environmental economics were applied when calculating the damages that the company had to pay for as a result of the accident. Another area where environmental economics is often applied is in the establishment of national parks, or in cases of exploitation of natural environments.

What is, then, the correct price to put on the environment? In principle there are two methods, either a contingent valuation (see further below), or an indirect measurement in which there is an attempt to find out how something else is valued – and which should be related to the environmental resource or problem that we are interested in putting a price on. Examples of this latter indirect method include using a person's travel costs as a measurement of how high he or she values visiting a particular recreational resort, or the differences in property prices as a measurement of how different housing areas are valued. Contingent valuation, the other main method, is based on people receiving direct questions concerning how much they would be prepared to pay for certain levels of environmental improvement or in order to avoid any further deterioration of the environment. The people who receive these questions make up the group (or a representative selection from that group) which is seen as the group that should decide on these matters, e.g. living in close proximity to a new road construction, or a whole country's population on the issue of an energy tax on fossil fuels. This involves various types of survey, e.g. questionnaires and telephone interviews, in which people are asked to give their preference to various choices; or asked how highly they value having, or being able to retain, certain environmentally related values – or avoiding environmental deterioration.

There are, of course, different kinds of values within environmental economics and it is common to differentiate between three so-called value components. These include:

> *utilization* of the current value e.g. a recreational landscape or clean air in a housing area for the present and the future; either directly e.g. hiking in the landscape or breathing clean air, or indirectly e.g. watching television programmes produced in that particular land-scape or regarding the clean air as a basic requirement for a healthy life;

> *opportunity* to possibly, sometime in the future, be able to utilise the current value (for personal gain or to benefit others) – the value of not excluding future opportunities;

> *existence value* which actually concerns the actual existence – intrinsic value – of the current state of the environment, even if there is no intention (or possibility) of gaining anything from the value or seeing no personal benefits in the avoidance of environmental deteriora-tion.

An additional important feature of environmental economics is the principle of 'common resources', which are resources that can be enjoyed by all people at all times. Environmental examples of common resources could be forests for recreation (in the cases when private ownership does not deny access), biological diversity, landscape sceneries, clean air and water. In practice, however, access to these 'resources' is often limited; this is due to what is known as either 'rivalry' or 'exclusion'. Rivalry is when one interest excludes the other, e.g. when land is being developed (property development) or when a mineral source is being mined: both these activities mean that other people can no longer use the resource in the same way. This can be compared to using the resources in a way which does not exclude other people, e.g. admiring beautiful scenery or using a forest footpath. But, even the latter example cannot be used by too many people for long periods of time without causing 'congestion' and damage, which in turn reduces the value of the resource (e.g. many people are of the opinion that when large groups of tourists visit national parks the value of the natural environment is diminished). The term exclusion is self-explanatory in that it addresses the possibilities of not allowing free access to the resource. If, for example, people do not have the right of public access, which allows the opportunity to enjoy outdoor recreational activities etc. on land that they do not own, it is possible to close off areas of natural beauty and charge a fee for those who wish to gain access. When a resource has a high level of rivalry (one person's usage excludes that of another) and a high level of exclusion (access can be denied) then it is no longer a 'common resource' and the situation becomes identical to that of ordinary private consumption e.g. purchasing items or renting property.

We conclude this section on the possibilities of using environmental economics by referring to a concrete example. It illustrates the great importance that the population of Sweden attaches to living in close proximity to a natural recreational area: in this case, wooded areas.[6] 1,000 people were selected at random and asked how far they lived from the nearest woods and how they would react if that distance was increased or reduced. The statistics showed that about 85% of all Swedes felt that it was important to live within walking distance (one kilometre) of a wooded area. The statistics also showed that approximately 40% would prefer to live closer to a wooded area (only 2% gave a positive response to having an increase in distance). The mean willingness to pay per person in order to avoid a 100% increase in the distance to the nearest woods (e.g. due to the local woods being chopped down for property development) was estimated to be a little less than $15 US a month. It was also noted in the research that the further away a person lived from a wooded area it became more likely that they would be willing to pay to avoid the distance becoming greater. This kind of result can be important for e.g. planning in cases such as deciding whether or not to preserve woodland areas lying in close proximity to urban centres or to build new roads or use land for property development.

6   Hörnsten & Fredman (2000).

Opposition and Criticism

In this section we will make a critical examination of the environmental economic strategies for introducing and maintaining sustainable development. There have been objections levelled at environmental economics in this respect; in some cases it has been a matter of principle and in others a matter of technology and methodology (partly as an element in the continual critical discussion of all science).

One criticism aimed at the founding ideas of environmental economics is that of not accepting the idea of pricing (commercialise) the environment.[7] Is it morally acceptable to regard, for example, clean air, clean water, biological diversity and the satisfaction of future generations in financial terms? We could note that the Swedish government includes the following in its new policy on nature conservation:

> to see a sea eagle fly in the archipelago, to experience an untouched forest or to fish on a quiet morning in a tranquil lake or bay are experiences which are extremely difficult to value in monetary terms.[8]

Is there possibly a risk that something crucial may be lost if we attach specific monetary values to e.g. natural experiences and species? What of altruism, common responsibilities, and democratic access to common resources? From an environmental economic perspective, it could e.g. be seen as problematic if people value a visit to a national park more highly than the amount of money they spend on the visit, as the national park then represents, to some extent, an unexploited resource which could be put to better use by e.g. the tourist industry or conservation authorities (e.g. charging a higher fee). But how reasonable is it to see such a valuation pattern as problematic? One point here is to what extent each individual should pay (from their own funds) for his or her consumption (e.g. visiting a national park), or whether or not it should been seen as a basic right for all people in which case the costs

---

7　This is a main element in the critics from advocates of ecological economics (see the start of this chapter) who argue that 'monetary reductionism' is an important aspect of neoclassical economics. See e.g. Daly (1996) and Söderbaum (2000).

8　Skr 2001/02:22-23.

involved would be financed by the taxpayer. Another aspect that remains unclear concerns the basic issue of the extent to which people are primarily driven by economic reason and rationality. In economics there is also an ongoing discussion that includes the importance of other values that affect human behaviour, such as social acceptance and moral judgements.

The main counter from environmental economists to this objection is that in modern industrial societies, most of the products and services are ultimately in some way valued in economic terms. Therefore it is of great importance to actively and consciously incorporate environmental aspects into economic strategies in order to avoid these values becoming totally sidelined in favour of short-term economic gain.

Environmental economics has also been criticised for not being able to offer the correct estimations. One side of this is the 'false exactness', which could be the result of the process of attempting to determine the value of such things as another species' right to live, or the importance of living in close proximity to nature. This false exactness can perhaps be as equally misleading as not putting a price on environmental resources at all. We can, for example, discuss the validity of the sum of almost $15 US per month from the above example about distances to wooded areas. Perhaps by rewording the questions in the survey (e.g. comparing the value of proximity to nature with hospital visits or a quick lunch) the figures would change drastically in either direction. To what extent is it possible to assume that people will have any well-founded opinion at all in this type of situation? They may be unable to relate to the alternatives that are offered in the survey, or an individual may have a complete change of mind if, for example, exposed to the information that would become available if e.g. the issue became a newsworthy political event. To what extent are people just plucking figures out of thin air – e.g. $15 – as nobody will ever ask them to pay directly, and they may very well have a hard time estimating such a quality in quantitative terms. To what extent are people actually prepared to face the reality of, e.g. a decline in health, if they only valued clean air as a low priority, or if they claimed that they were prepared to pay quite large sums from their income to avoid the extinction of a certain species of insect in a South American rainforest?

If we approach this critique from another angle, we can see the risk of results being distorted since, in general, certain things are much easier to attach a monetary value to than others (cf. above, the value components user value and existence value). Is it really possible to apply a universal yardstick – money – to such a diversity of details; is this not a case of confusing issues and attempting to solve problems by merely presenting statistics? Are not democratic and legal institutions/processes more suitable for the thorough deliberations that are necessary when dealing with such subtle differences between values? The environmental economic argument opposing this criticism is that money can be a quite clear and easy-to-manage yardstick when dealing with environmental values that are often hard to define, and where environmental problems are mainly diffuse, global and affect more than one generation (cf. chapter three). A requirement for monetary valuation would then be that it is carried out in a framework and according to goals established with the help of democratic and legal institutions.

The fact that environmental economists are engaged in responding to these criticisms has brought about improvements in surveys and interviews, clarifying situations where choices are made, the use of opportunity costs etc. They have, of course, had a harder time dealing with the critique that addresses the very issue of monetary valuation, but have pointed out that other methods of valuing hard-to-measure and hard-to-compare phenomena also have their disadvantages. For example, is it only the groups with good resources, e.g. economic resources (!), that will dominate a more traditional political or legal process with regard to the evaluation of environmental issues?

Economic Discussions: Necessary But Not Sufficient

We shall conclude this chapter by broadening the somewhat specific methodological and conceptual perspectives of environmental economics. We will here attempt to address the founding economic aspects of sustainable development by highlighting the classic case of what has been erroneously been called 'the tragedy of the commons'[9]. The original story tells of a situation where an unrestricted number of livestock was allowed to graze in a commonly owned pasture. Eventually the area became overused and its value as pasture declined to below its original value. The basic idea is that each farmer who puts his livestock to graze sees the addition of an extra animal as being economically rational to himself, even though it is apparent that the pasture eventually will be unable to sustain the large number of livestock that will result from such action, and thereby also to sustain its value as pasture. If instead the farmers had agreed amongst themselves to restrict the number of livestock allowed on the pasture, each individual farmer would have been better off. The story of 'the tragedy of the commons' is quite frequently used as a general illustration of the problems involved in how to correctly manage common resources such as the atmosphere, or the fish in the world's oceans.

However, it was said above that it was wrong to call this story a tragedy of the commons and the reason is that it is rather a story of the tragic use of a resource with open access. Extensive research has shown that for each common resource: pastures, forests, lakes etc. that has been commonly managed by, for example, a village, it is likely that there will also be very well developed procedures to avoid over-exploitation. Such procedures have included regulations on e.g. how much livestock or fishing equipment each person may put in. The attempts to maintain long-term sustainability have also included quorum community meetings and other forms of common decision- making, social control, and various social institutions for punishment. Let us now draw the first general conclusion from the so called tragedy of the commons example, namely that there is a need for continuous, critical research to serve as a watchdog to avoid quickly drawn conclusions from studies of specific contexts and/or specific historical periods. In relation to this, two risks need to be observed. Firstly, there is the risk of romanticising a specific alternative that contrasts with the current perception of what is regarded as an unsatisfactory and unsustainable development (e.g. having romantic visions of the hunter-gatherer period; see chapter one). Secondly, there is the risk of underestimating

---

9   Hardin (1968), cf. e.g. Ostrom (1992).

people in other cultures and other historical contexts and their abilities and skills in dealing with environmental resource issues. Unfortunately it often assumed that wisdom and rationality are features of the industrialised nations alone (one important original purpose of the tragedy of the commons was to advocate the necessity of private ownership in the striving to manage contemporary environmental problems). Rather than illustrating problems with common ownership, the so-called tragedy of the commons example effectively depicts the devastating effects when no one (individual or community) considers themselves the owners of (and responsible for) a common resource.

The case of the pasture, above, quite clearly illustrates the need to avoid situations where resources such as e.g. the atmosphere or the oceans of the world are considered as open access resources; instead the case can be interpreted as indicating the need for a higher degree of collective responsibility for such resources. It is therefore necessary – in the cases where privatisation and allocation are not suitable – to reform the regulations for ownership and allow the resources to resemble the regulations for 'common property'. As was pointed out earlier, this would involve establishing suitable arenas for discussion and debate in order to produce the necessary political means. This process would lead to the practical application of policies such as planning, imposing regulations, supervisory tasks and sanctions etc. The fact that individual economic gain is not the only item on the agenda in a discussion about managing common resources is quite apparent to most of us. Where social control in a local community is concerned, e.g. with regard to grazing, status, ideological arguments (moral, religious etc.), and where there is a need for cooperation in other areas, the actions of the individual or the group are often very important (and here the institutional economist would agree).

Another general conclusion that can be drawn from the so called tragedy of the commons example – and one very closely linked to the general theme of this book – is the importance of democratic discussions and communication as a necessary element in all aspects of sustainable development. Take, for example, a village meeting in a pre-industrial society, which was a necessary arena for dialogue where issues like the need for regulations, concern for over-exploitation or border violations could be addressed. When issues like that are concerned environmental economists often refer to the game about the so-called prisoners' dilemma. Imagine the situation where two people have committed a crime together and have been arrested without having had the opportunity to work out a story. They are both faced with the situation of knowing that if one of them denies all charges but the other admits to everything, then the person who refuses to cooperate will receive a much harder sentence. If they both deny involvement in the crime they will probably receive lighter sentences for other less serious crimes, and finally, if they both admit to the crime, they will both probably receive harsher punishments. This implies that the most rational choice for them (confessing) will lead to a considerably worse result for both of them (they receive the severe sentence). Had the two criminals had time to cooperate, they would both deny the charges and receive the minimal punishment. If we apply this scenario to environmental issues it involves the question of needing to know if others will contribute towards solving problems, which is, of course, the best solution. If the situation is such that one does not know to what extent other people will take part, then it seems more rational for individuals not to e.g. recycle household refuse, and e.g. continue to drive their car to work instead of car-pooling or using public transport.

Economics and Sustainable Development: A Summary

In this chapter we have focused on environmental economics as a way of defining and controlling environmentally related issues. However, as was initially pointed out, this is merely an example of a scientific viewpoint and methodology for the implementation of sustainable development. It is but one perspective, which can and should be compared with the many other perspectives and models, and be supplemented in various ways. Comparisons can be made with other economic perspectives e.g. natural resource economics, ecological economics and institutional economics, as mentioned earlier in the chapter, or with the previous chapters' perspectives on ecology, ethics and politics. In addition to these, there are a great many other perspectives which have not been included in this book, due to a lack of space e.g. public health, social planning, regional development, law etc. All these have, of course, their own key theories, concepts and methods, which are employed in different ways when addressing the issues that affect sustainable development.

It is however fair to guess that economic debates and environmental economic methods will come to play an important role in future discussions on sustainable development. Below are some critical aspects that are important to bear in mind:

– the importance of not viewing people and society as exclusively driven by economic gain (the so called "economic man"; even though it is often a crucial factor in decision making), but to also pay attention to the importance of other motives, e.g. existential values and social acceptance;

– the importance of investigating the value components, values of the groups and the time perspectives involved in various estimations in environmental economics (e.g. to what extent the needs of future generations are given priority – discounting models are often used in relation to future generations, as technological development is then assumed to allow them more opportunities than we have today);

– the risk of false exactness and systematic bias of results due to difficulties in measuring and comparing various environmental resources.

But also it seems necessary to conclude this chapter by drawing the reader's attention to the following noteworthy explanations as to why there should be a continued interest in the methods of environmental economics as an important complement in the work with sustainable development:

– in market oriented societies there is, of course, the risk that environmental and resource issues will not receive any attention at all if they are not valued in monetary terms;

– the research on a 'green' GNP, which attempts to estimate the increase and decrease in various natural and environmentally related resources (e.g. fish populations or mineral assets), will possibly enable a supplementary (or even correctional) method of comparison to conventional calculations of a country's products and services;

– another important issue for further development is the green tax reform method, in favour of e.g. increasing taxation on the use of non-renewable resources and decreasing taxation on labour;–

– the need to use environmental economics as a basis on which to develop better methods for what actually inspires action towards sustainable development with regard to e.g. environmental taxes, fees and reward systems, and thereby incentives for e.g. choosing environmentally friendly consumer goods;

– attentiveness to cost effectiveness can maximise resources employed in working towards sustainable development (e.g. it might perhaps be better to invest in sanitation measures in the rivers of a neighbouring country located in the same catchment area).

Further Reading

Some titles which offer a comprehensive insight into environmental economics include: *Environmental Economics in Theory and Practice* (Hanley, N.; Shogren, J.F. & White, B., Oxford University Press, 1997); Barry Field's *Environmental Economics: An Introduction* (Mc Graw-Hill, Second Edition, 1997); and Ian Hodge's *Environmental Economics: Individual Incentives and Public Choices* (St Martin's Press, 1995). Among the titles which take a more advanced approach on the subject we could note: *Natural Resource and Environmental Economics* (Perman, R.; McGilvray, J.; Ma, Y. & Common , M., Longman, 1999).

Other Reference Literature

Daly, Herman E. (1996). *Beyond Growth: The Economics of Sustainable Development*. Boston: Beacon Press.

Fredman, Peter (1997). En Dag i skogen 200:- (A Day in the Woods 200 SEK) *Forskning & Framsteg*, No. 2 s. 26–31.

Friman, Eva (2002). *No Limits: The 20th Century Discourse of Economic Growth*. Umeå, Sweden: Umeå University.

Hahn, Thomas (Ed.) (1997). *Miljöekonomi och ekologisk ekonomi – en teoretisk introduktion* (Environmental Economics and Ecological Economics – A Theoretical Introduction). Uppsala: Småskriftserien No. 101, Inst. f. ekonomi, SLU.

Hardin, Garret (1968). The Tragedy of the Commons. *Science* Vol. 162, pp. 1243–1248.

Hörnsten, Lisa & Fredman, Peter (2000). On the Distance to Recreational Forests in Sweden. *Landscape and Urban Planning,* Vol. 51, pp. 1–10.

Kvaløy, Sigmund (1987). Norwegian Ecophilosophy and Ecopolitics and their Influence from Buddhism. In: Sandell, Klas (Ed.), *Buddhist Perspectives on the Ecocrisis.* Buddhist Publication Society, Wheel series, No. 346/ 348, Kandy, Sri Lanka, pp. 49–72.

Ostrom, Elinor. (1992). *Governing the Commons: The Evolution of Institutions for Collective Action.* Cambridge: Cambridge University Press.

Schumacher, Ernst Friedrich (1973). *Small is Beautiful: Economics as if People Mattered.* New York.

Söderbaum, Peter (2000). *Ecological Economics: A Political Economics Approach to Environment and Development.* London: Earthscan.

Skr 2001/02. *En samlad naturvårdspolitik.* Regerings skrivelse 2001/02:173. Regeringskansliet, Stockholm (A Comprehensive Nature Conservation Policy. Government Report 2001/02:173). Stockholm.

Öckerman, Anders & Friman, Eva (Ed.) (2003). *Hela världen: Samhälleliga och kulturella perspektiv på miljökrisen* (The Whole World: Social and Cultural Perspectives on the Environmental Crises). Lund: Studentlitteratur.

In Part I we showed that humankind's approach to and interaction with the natural world has changed dramatically during the course of time. Thus humankind's relationship with the natural world is something that is connected to learning. The way we relate to the natural world and the social development, both as individuals and members of society, can therefore be influenced by the way we are educated. The purpose of Part III is to describe how the learning and teaching process can be understood, and based on that understanding present a number of applications and models that can be used in ESD teaching.

One important insight from Part II is that environmental- and development issues can be understood in terms of knowledge, of values and attitudes, and of politics (democracy). In this part of the book we will describe the learning and teaching process in relation to these three dimensions, i.e. we will try to describe the teaching and learning process in terms of knowledge; morals and ethics; and democracy.

In the Introduction we suggested that competence to teach on the subject of sustainable development consists of:

- knowledge of environmental problems and sustainable development,
- theoretical knowledge of teaching and learning,
- practical knowledge and teaching skills (experience).

We also stressed that competence lies in the ability to integrate this knowledge and these skills when planning and teaching. This part is dedicated to the second and third type of knowledge and the ability to integrate the three different kinds of knowledge.

Part III is structured in the following way: First of all (chapter eight) we make a clarification of ESD by comparing the differences between ESD and other selective traditions within environmental education in schools. To be able to evaluate ESD in relation to the other traditions we turn, in chapter nine, to the democratic elements of education as a common point of reference. In the two following chapters (chapters ten and eleven) we look at both the learning and teaching perspectives on ESD. The final chapter (chapter twelve) contains three teaching models which can be used in ESD. These models are a result of an integration of the three types of knowledge mentioned above.

8 Selective Traditions Within Environmental Education

In this chapter we will attempt to present an introductory clarification of what education for sustainable development actually represents: what are the specific characteristics of Education for Sustainable Development (ESD)? What is new and what has already been accomplished in schools? A method of finding the answers to these questions is to compare education for sustainable development with earlier forms of environmental education.

Environmental education has clearly undergone changes during the years and is still approached differently in schools today. Research into the history of school subjects has shown that different traditions of how content and methods are selected in education are present within different areas of school studies. These traditions can therefore be termed "selective traditions"[1]. These selective traditions represent a number of solutions as to what constitutes the best form of teaching within a subject, and also include different approaches in both the choice and organisation of content as well as the choice of teaching methods. Like most established traditions, selective traditions often function as an unobtrusive frame of reference, which suggests that one's personal understanding of what constitutes a good education is usually part of a general consensus on the matter. This usually results in new target proposals etc. being greatly influenced by frames of reference within current selective traditions. Here there is a great risk that new ideas and goals will never be realised. It is therefore important

---

1   The term "selective tradition" was originally developed by Williams (1973) to underline the fact that a certain approach towards knowledge and a certain educational praxis is always selected within the framework of a specific culture. The regular patterns of the selective processes that develop over time form a selective tradition. For studies of different selective traditions within specific school subjects see e.g. Fensham, (1998); Goodson, (1987) and Östman, (1995).

to be aware of the traditions that exist within a subject or field of study in order to make critical and conscious choices of educational content and methods.

Environmental Approach and Educational Philosophy

To a great extent, a person's specific view on environmental issues – their individual *environmental approach* – influences the way they approach and conduct environmental education. At a deeper level, this concerns how one perceives the character, extent and seriousness of environmental- and developmental problems, as well as how much importance one attaches to protecting the environment, taking part in environmental debates and the position one takes in environmental politics. We have already discussed the wide range of approaches to these issues in previous chapters. If we look at the conflicting interests which can appear in environmental issues, it is easy to appreciate that people adopt opposing positions in the range of environmentally related topics depending on their perspectives, values, intentions and interests. The aspect of environmental problems seen in terms of ecological, ethical, economical or political questions has also been addressed in earlier chapters. An important aspect of how we perceive the environment includes asking which of the above perspectives we consider to be the most important.

An opinion of the 'correct' approach towards environmental education is also determined by how one perceives education in general; we can label this *educational philosophy*. Educational philosophy encompasses general ideas on the role and purpose of schools in society, as well as that which directly affects the teaching process. One way of structuring an understanding of educational philosophy is to start from the three main questions in education: *why?* – the motives of education; *what?* – the content of education; and *how?* – the method used in education. These questions can be problematised based on several different perspectives. From a student perspective, it concerns the learning aspects e.g. how the student

perceives the teaching and what the implications and consequences of the teaching are –which in turn depends on the situation and context as well as the background and experience of the
student. From a teaching perspective, it is mainly a case of the
choices of motive, content and method the teacher makes. Here we
will (mainly) address the teacher perspective as a point of departure
and, more specifically, look at the three main questions in the education process in the following way:

- On a social level, the *why* question addresses the main function
  of the school – the purpose the school serves in society. There is
  a basic difference of opinion in this question between those who
  regard the school as an institution which supports continuity in
  society, in the sense that it preserves and cultivates basic norms,
  values, viewpoints and knowledge; and those who suggest that
  the primary function of schools is to create change in society
  through questioning and critically assessing that which is considered habitual and taken for granted. The *why* question encompasses, therefore, visions of an ideal society – not least it considers how we see the role of the school in a democracy. Based on
  these broad standings on the role of the school in society, it is
  possible to observe differing opinions on the motives of teaching
  in various subjects and the levels of aptitude students should
  attain.
- The *what* question looks into the choice of content and on what
  particular grounds certain content is chosen. There is a great deal
  that can be included in teaching, even within the parameters of
  school policies – the question is: what is the most important and
  central in each case? This question is concerned with reasons
  why the teacher (and students) select a certain type of material,
  which also indicates that it is a question which concerns the
  teacher's view on whether or not knowledge is true, valid and
  useful (i.e. whether there is only one truth or several truths on
  the same issue; if it is only the models and terminology of science
  that are valid or if common sense and practical knowledge are
  also important aspects of our understanding of the world).
- The *how* question deals with the choice of work methods and
  approaches. A central question is: how can students effectively
  develop and achieve the goals which have been established in

the curriculum? The how question includes, therefore, understanding how the actual learning process takes place as well as how students are perceived e.g. whether a student is seen as a passive receiver of information who requires external motivation (e.g. qualifications), or whether the student is regarded as active and knowledge seeking with his/her own motivation. An important aspect of this question is how democracy is manifested in the teaching process, or to what degree the students not only participate but are also involved in the planning and realisation of the lessons.

A logical and systematic way of considering the above questions can be said to represent a specific educational philosophy. A specific educational philosophy is thus to be seen as a clear and coherent approach to the purpose and role of education in society, as well as a specific view to the mechanisms of, and the conditions for, the teaching and learning process. During the latter part of the 20th Century and the first years of the 21st Century, the debate on education has been dominated by three educational philosophies: *essentialism, progressivism* and *reconstructivism*. These educational philosophies are explained in brief below.[2]

- *Essentialism* states that the content of the education is to be based on the sciences. Here it is the actual subject that has priority and the teaching is based on instilling adapted scientific terminology and models. The role of the teacher is that of an expert in the subject, who has the task of transferring knowledge and facts to the students.
- *Progressivism* places the students in a central position. The teaching is organised around the needs and interests of the students. The choice of teaching methods is also given a great deal of priority, and the emphasis is on cooperation and problem solving as important aspects of the learning process. Student knowledge is developed through first hand experience of the natural world and society.

---

2   Descriptions of different educational philosophies were originally formulated by Brameld (1950) and Kneller (1972).

- *Reconstructivism* emphasises the role of the school in the demo-cratic development of a future ideal society. A lot of attention is given to the teaching content and the viewpoints represented by the content. The objective is that students learn how to critically evaluate a wide range of different alternatives.

The Characteristics of the Selective Traditions of Environmental Education

Analyses of various official documents and policy documents for environmental education in schools have shown that there are at least three different selective traditions of environmental educa-tion.[3] We will label these environmental teaching traditions based on their main orientations: *Fact-based environmental education, Normative environmental education* and *Education for sustainable development.*

These three traditions of environmental education describe dif-ferent ways of understanding the correct form of environmental education that has developed in schools. Traditions in environmen-tal education can be seen as historical accounts of environmental teaching, and can be accredited with constituting a part of the development where one tradition is based on the other, although studies have shown that these three traditions are all present in schools today. The purpose of clarifying these traditions is to estab-lish some sort of reference point that can be applied when discuss-

---

3   These text analyses are carried out by e.g. Östman 1995 and 1999. The categori-zation of environmental education into three separate traditions has also been applied in the Swedish National Agency for Education's evaluation of environ-mental education in schools. That evaluation established the division of three separate traditions and demonstrated that they were both logical and coherent. The evaluation also demonstrated that all three traditions are present in schools today. The full result of the evaluation is available in Swedish in the National Agency's report: *Miljöundervisning för en hållbar utveckling i svensk skola (Environ-mental education and education for sustainable development in the Swedish school system)*, (2001), a popular version of the evaluation can be found in the National Agency's reference material *Hållbar utveckling i skolan (Sustainable development in schools)*, (2002).

ing teaching on the subject of the environment and sustainable development. They can be seen as alternatives to reflect on, oppose or support when planning lessons or formulating ideas. Here the question arises with regard to where we ourselves actually stand in relation to these traditions, and what we actually aim to achieve in our teaching.

It is important to point out here that the accounts of these traditions are in summary form and have been edited in order to make them clearer. As we are aware, reality is considerably more complex than our descriptions of it – there are infinite details to acknowledge in the practicalities of teaching and people are not always logical in their actions. In practice, teaching is always made up of a combination of different perspectives; although most teachers usually remain within the boundaries of one tradition.

We will now take a closer look at the characteristics of the three traditions of environmental education, with reference to their roots in educational philosophy as well as how environmental and developmental problems are perceived.

Fact -based Environmental Education

The fact-based tradition took shape during the development of environmental education in the 1960s, but became firmly established during the 1970s.

Environmental Approach

Fact-based environmental education is based on the approach that environmental problems are questions of science, and more specifically questions of ecology. It is based on the belief that science will solve all problems in this area. Environmental problems are therefore regarded as being knowledge-based problems which can be resolved by carrying out more research and supplying more information to the public. It is, therefore, the scientists (mainly natural scientists) who are expected to solve these environmental problems that are seen as being unfortunate side effects of the development of society, the main cause of which is industrial production. The aim is to curb these side effects of the exploitation of the world's natural resources in such a way that secures the future of human prosperity and development. From an environmentally ethical perspective, this tradition is in agreement with the beliefs of modern anthropocentrism (see chapter 5). The natural world is considered as being separate from humankind and it is the task of humans to control it. The natural world is valued depending on how it can best serve humans.

Educational philosophy

From an educational philosophy point of view, this tradition lies closest to *essentialism*. In order to gain an understanding of environmental problems, the teaching process focuses on knowledge within the actual discipline. When dealing with environmental problems, the focus is on the study of scientific facts concerning current localised problems, their background and causes.

The focus in the lessons is centred on conveying scientific facts and concepts which have been adapted for educational purposes. Based on these supposedly objective facts, the students are then expected to draw independent conclusions and act on them. The most usual method of teaching in schools is teacher-led lessons. If it is necessary (or possible), laboratory tests or other practical experiments are carried out in order to illustrate particular phenomena. Field trips and other excursions also take place to a certain extent. All teaching is mainly carried out within the school's traditional subjects. Student participation takes place to the extent that the teacher observes students' attitudes and opinions and then incorporates them into future lesson plans.

Normative Environmental Education

During the 1980s, a new orientation in the social debate on environmental problems emerged (see chapter two). This development led to a challenge of the fact-based approach to environment and environmental education.

Environmental Approach

Within this tradition, environmental problems are primarily a question of values. The problems are looked upon as a conflict between humans and nature. This conflict affects human values, and environmental problems are resolved by adopting environmentally friendly values. In order to do this effectually, people must adjust the whole of society according to the knowledge and information gathered on the natural world e.g. well grounded ecological models, thermodynamic theories etc. Scientific knowledge is therefore regarded as promoting certain normative, prescribed values, which are acted on accordingly. Experts from various fields of science should, therefore, be those who advise and direct people in terms of how they should approach environmental issues, and what environmental values they should adopt. As a consequence, the goals in the development of society are seen as being clear and unambiguous: the environmentally friendly society is the ideal society. Similarly environmentally friendly values and actions are also considered to be good. From an environmentally ethical point of view, humans are seen as a part of nature and should therefore adapt to its conditions. More specifically, ethical logic can be taken from late-modern anthropocentrism, as well as biocentrism and ecocentrism (see chapter five).

Educational Philosophy

The primary goal in this approach to environmental education is that students are taught to develop environmentally-friendly values and behaviour based on scientific knowledge. A lot of attention is focused on developing the ability to form and defend a standpoint that is based on scientific fact. The reference point for this approach is the idea that a strong, almost causal, relationship exists between knowledge, values and behaviour; with knowledge in e.g. fundamental ecological conditions, students will naturally begin to act more responsibly towards the environment. A central aspect is the development of practical skills i.e. the ability to put into practice what has been studied and discussed in theory. From this approach, the teaching method can be said to aspire to encouraging humans to adapt to nature in order that the ecological balance and the continued health of humankind can be secured for future years. This approach is often characterised by social criticism.

The content of the education consists to a large extent of subjects within the natural sciences; however, the social sciences also play a significant role. The educational content is partly organised in a thematic way, in which several teachers cooperate. The lesson content includes current and local issues, with global problems and future consequences also being addressed. In addition to environmental issues, resource distribution and population growth are also included. Although the lessons are based on scientific facts, values and emotional aspects are included.

To ensure that the lessons achieve the intended objectives, a great deal of attention is given to work methods and using student reference points that are based on their experiences and attitudes. The lessons are usually group-based activities, where students look for facts and information themselves, or are practically activated in other ways. Field trips are also part of this approach, as certain aspects of the lessons require first hand experience. The teacher and students carry out lesson planning together.

Together with a focus on problem solving, the combination of scientific facts and practically active students makes this tradition appear as a combination of essentialism and progressivism, which can be called *progressentialism*.

Education for Sustainable Development (ESD)

This tradition was developed during the 1990s, in connection with the Rio conference in 1992, as well as the debate and movement linked with Agenda 21. In recent years, the debate on the globalisation of the economy has, with all probability, had a certain amount of influence on this type of teaching. Increasing uncertainty on environmental issues and the growing amount of differing opinions in environmental debates are central points of departure in this tradition.

Environmental Approach

In this tradition, environment- and development issues are identified as being conflicts between different human interests. This implies that environmental problems are seen as political and moral issues. Different groups of people with equally different viewpoints and values have their own opinions of what constitutes an environmental- and/or a developmental problem; they also have differing views on how serious these problems are. As science is confined to supplying facts, it is not regarded as an ultimate source of guidance concerning the political and moral aspects of environment- and development issues.

The environmental theme is broadened considerably and is linked to the whole spectrum of social development. The environmental concept is therefore replaced with the concept of sustainable development, which encompasses ecological as well as economic and social sustainability.

The conflict-based perspective of ESD, with ties to the whole spectrum of social development, places the democratic process in focus. The opinions and values of all people are regarded as being equally relevant when determining the courses of action in environmental- and development issues. The democratic debate can be said to centre on the discussion of the 'good' society and quality of life, and how that can be achieved in the present and maintained in the future. No single environmental ethic is prioritised in this approach; here each alternative receives critical examination.

Educational Philosophy

The aim of this approach to environmental education is to give students the opportunity to learn knowledge and skills so that they can actively and critically evaluate different perspectives of environmental- and developmental issues. In this way the students develop the ability to engage in democratic discussions concerning how best to create a sustainable society and a sustainable world. This aspect suggests that the lessons have a *reconstructivist* character.

The teaching content includes the relationship between local and global problems as well as between the past, present and future. The focus is on sustainable development and the related topics of economics, society and ecology. Sustainable development is a recurring theme in all education, due to its total integration.

The varied character and problems encountered in various aspects of the lessons indicate that methods of approach are also varied. Discussing the wide range of viewpoints is considered to be an important aspect of the lessons. Fact-based studies investigate the various standpoints on this development as well as the various conflicts existing between each party. This implies that natural and social sciences, in addition to experience-based, moral and aesthetical perspectives, feature in the lesson content. This indicates that pluralism is a reference point in the lessons. Under the supervision of the teacher, students are themselves responsible for lesson plans and realisation.

A Summary of Environmental Education Traditions

In summarizing the three selective traditions in environmental education in table form, we are able to identify a number of significant differences between them. The characteristics of the different traditions with regard to *approach to the environment* can be summarised according to the following table:

Tradition of Environmental Education	Fact-based Environmental Education	Normative Environmental Education	Education for Sustainable Development
Perspective on Environmental problems	Environmental problems are scientific knowledge-based in character and are resolved by means of research and gathering information	Environmental problems are value questions which can be resolved by exerting an influence on people's attitudes and behaviour	Environmental problems are political issues which should be dealt with democratically
The Cause of Environmental Problems	An unforeseen result of production and resource exploitation in society	A conflict between society and the laws of nature	Conflicts between humans' wide range of achievement goals

Tradition of Environmental Education	Fact-based Environmental Education	Normative Environmental Education	Education for Sustainable Development
Assessment of Specialists	Advice is sourced from experts in natural sciences	Experts from various disciplines are consulted even in value qestions	All people are considered equal in deciding the outcome of political issues
The Goals of Environmental Measures	Industrial production and the standard of living are the main priority	Health and survival	Increase quality of life, even for future generations
Humankind's Relationship with the Natural World	Humans are separate from nature; the natural world should be under human control	Humans are an element of the natural world and should live according to its laws	Humans and nature are bound in a cycle of events and transitions

If we read the table from left to right we are able to see opinions on environmental issues ranging from a clear and unambiguous scientific problem to a viewpoint which is all encompassing as well as being more diffuse and abstract. As a result we can see that the conflict perspective is enhanced, the political and moral perspectives become more tangible, and environmental- and developmental questions become more closely linked with democratic issues.

These differences can be compared with those in the original reference point in educational philosophy, which is held by each respective tradition of environmental education. This variance is seen most clearly when we summarise and compare the *goals*:

Tradition of Environmental Education	Fact-based Environmental Education	Normative Environmental Education	Education for Sustainable Development
The goal of environmental education	Students receive knowledge of environmental problems by learning scientific facts	Students actively develop environmentally friendly values, primarily based on knowledge of ecology	Students develop their ability to critically evaluate various alternative perspectives on environmental- and developmental problems

By referring to these goals we can be more specific about identifying and summarising the important differentiations in the *content* and *teaching methods* of environmental education:

Environmental Education Traditions	Fact-based Environmental Education	Normative Environmental Education	Education for Sustainable Development
Political and moral reference point	A-political and a-moral	Morally and politically norma-tive	Morally and politically critical
Central subjects and areas of knowledge	Natural sciences	Natural science and aspects of social science	Economical, social and eco-logical perspec-tives as well as ethical and aes-thetical aspects
Organisation of lessons and teach-ing materials	Separate subjects	Thematic	Integrated
Time perspective	Present	Present and future	Future in rela-tion to the past and present
Geographical per-spective	Local	Local and global	Local, regional and global incor-porated
Main Method of Teaching	Factual informa-tion from teacher to student	Student active in the develop-ment of know-ledge and values	Critical discus-sions based on a number of alter-natives
Students	Passive	Active	Active and critical
Planning and Democracy	Teacher plans based on observa-tions and experi-ence of students' input	Teacher and students plan together	Students plan under teacher supervision

If we compare Fact-based environmental education with Education for sustainable development we can see that environmental educa-tion, from a content point of view, has been expanded not only in aspects of time and space but also in scale; more school subjects are now involved. One interpretation could be that this type of educa-tion has become more focused on dealing with a complex reality –

attempting to grasp patterns and systems. Moreover, the lessons have become oriented towards the future and now have a larger input of political and moral perspectives in environmental and resource issues.

If the fact-based tradition concentrates on *results* in the form of learning specific scientific facts, and the normative tradition concentrates on *effects* in the form of environmentally friendly attitudes and behavioural patterns, then education for sustainable development is more concerned with being a catalyst of *processes*. Reading from left to right, the table demonstrates that students develop a more active and unrestricted role; this progression matches the lessons and approach towards environmental education developing a more critical and investigative character.

Reference Literature

Brameld, Theodore (1950). *Patterns of Educational Philosophy. A Democratic Interpretation*. New York: World Book Company.

Fensham, Peter (1998). *Development and Dilemmas in Science Education*. London: The Falmer Press.

Goodson, Ivor (1987). *School Subjects and Curriculum Change. Studies in Curriculum History*. London: The Falmer Press.

Kneller, George F. (1972). *Introduction to the Philosophy of Education*. New York: Wiley.

Östman, Leif (1995). *Socialisation och mening. No-utbildning som politiskt och miljömoraliskt problem. (Socialization and Meaning. Science education as a political and environmental-ethical problem)*. (Uppsala Studies in Education 61). Stockholm: Almqvist & Wiksell International.

Östman, Leif (1999). Förnuft i utbildning och medier: att klargöra våra syften (Reason in education and media: clarifying our purposes). In Carl Anders Säfström & Leif Östman (Eds.), *Textanalys(Text analysis)* (pp. 263–282). Lund: Studentlitteratur.

Swedish National Agency for Education (2001). *Miljöundervisning och utbildning för hållbar utveckling i svensk skola (Environmental education and education for sustainable development in the Swedish school system)*. Report number 00:3041.

Swedish National Agency for Education (2002). *Hållbar utveckling i skolan (Sustainable development in school)*. Stockholm: Liber.

Williams, Raymond (1973). Base and Superstructure in Marxist Cultural Theory. *New Left Review, 82*, pp. 3–16.

9 Environmental Education from a Democratic Perspective

Evaluating the Alternatives

How can we most effectively evaluate the three different approaches to environmental education described in the previous chapter? Even though the three alternatives can be seen as a historical development of environmental education, it does not necessarily imply that education for sustainable development is 'better' than e.g. fact-based environmental education. None of these three traditions can in themselves be regarded as being either better or worse than the next when one considers that each respective tradition has developed different perspectives of determining what is a 'good' approach to environmental education. There is, clearly, no objective method of establishing what is 'right', since what is considered correct always stems from certain perspectives, intentions or pre-determined interests and values. We simply see things differently.

Making the 'right' choice is far from straightforward, even if one consults official documents since these are always the product of political compromise between varying interests and are consequently open to a certain amount of interpretation. Additionally, teachers who read the documents tend to apply their own perspectives and ultimately contribute their own subjective opinions to the content of the syllabi and curricula.

It is only when we see environmental education in relation to an established norm that we can begin to evaluate different alternatives. In order for such a norm to be accepted with any validity, it must be done so by the majority of people. Democracy is one such norm. If we agree that one of the most important roles of schools is to reinforce the process of democracy in society, and that the democratic process is fundamental in resolving environmental issues, this norm will accordingly provide a suitable background for evaluating the alternatives in environmental education. In this chapter we will discuss the democratic starting points and the democratic conclusions of the three traditions.

The Democratic Dimensions of Education

One starting point for the line of reasoning we will follow here is that the democratic perspective on environmental issues does not only constitute a perspective – democracy is a constant dimension in education. It is our aim to present a way of approaching the democratic dimension of education which can be useful in this respect.

Society expects that schools take the democratic aspect of education very seriously – most people would agree that one of the most important functions of schools is to maintain and develop the democratic society. This task can be presented as two separate goals. The first is to instil in the growing generation both the knowledge and desire to *participate in the debates* which form our society. A closer study of environmental education similarly suggests that schools ought to provide the necessary encouragement that will allow future generations to feel inclined to actively participate in the social debates on environmental- and developmental issues. The second goal is to ensure that the schools are managed in a democratic way, which, among other aspects, requires that students should be included in decisions concerning lesson content, methods of approach etc. This is referred to as *participation* in decision-making.

The goal of participation in decision-making is attributed with more significance if we consider that environmental education and education for sustainable development can be seen as being political in nature: each choice made concerning the content in environmental education lessons indicates that students are offered access to certain areas of knowledge and opinions, whereas others are excluded. This means that the choice of content etc. can have an important effect on how students continue to formulate their future plans and lives. With this in mind, it strongly suggests that the schools' objectives, as far as participation is concerned, are absolutely central in the matter of selecting educational approaches.

This democratic perspective on environmental education and education for sustainable development illustrates one of the most central dilemmas confronting teachers. It concerns how education can encourage students to come to certain desirable conclusions on the environment and sustainable development at the same time as allowing them the freedom to express their opinions. This freedom happens to be fundamental in the goals of democracy: a credible democratic approach in the teaching process must include the opportunity for students to form their own opinions on all environmental and development issues. We do not intend to suggest a solution to this dilemma, however, as we feel that this is a matter that requires individual deliberation. On the other hand, we will attempt to present an outline which allows for a qualified discussion on the subject.

Education on Environmental and Sustainable Development is Political

Compulsory education is arguably society's largest institution that the state has control of. It might also be fair to say that it is one of the state's most effective resources for shaping society for future generations.

As the majority of children in many countries take part in compulsory state education, politicians and political groups who act upon, and are responsible for education legislation, official reports, national tests, continuation courses etc., strive to control the areas of knowledge, values, interests and points of view that the new members of society are exposed to during the course of their education. Schools are therefore institutions in which there is a great deal of disagreement between a number of social groups, all with different opinions and values concerning the orientation of the school and ultimately the world view offered to people who attend the school. Based on this perspective, the main purpose of environmental education and education for sustainable development can be formulated as an attempt to cultivate a standpoint on the environment and sustainable development for future generations and, as a result, create a specific future society.

Official reports and documents are, to some degree, vaguely worded. This is due to the fact that curricula and syllabi are the results of political compromise. Parliamentary committees formulate the guidelines for official documents and decisions . Before any documents can be presented, the committee – which can be made up of representatives from several political parties – must have already agreed on the content. The formulations are therefore often made in such a way that all members of the committee can agree on them.

The resulting vague content makes it possible for all those involved in schools, teacher training and the production of teaching materials to make arbitrary interpretations concerning the approach, values and opinions that schools convey to students.

The people who actually work in schools have, therefore, a real opportunity to participate and influence in ensuring a high standard of education on the environment and sustainable development. However, that which is considered a 'high standard education' varies according to our values (e.g. environmental morals) and interests, and can lead to further discussions and conflicts on the correct interpretation of the official documents. In practice, those who have the power to appoint people who are involved in the decision making process itself decide whether an education is good or not.

Based on the above, it is possible to draw the following conclusion: the structuring of education – on all levels – is fundamentally a political process (here politics is the process of influencing other people's opportunities to shape and direct their lives). Even the duties of teachers – from interpreting official documents to actual teaching – are political. The easiest way of illustrating this is that each text and each lesson contains a selection of what is to be said about e.g. the natural world and our relationship with it. From a student perspective, this means that the opportunities to shape their own lives depend to a great extent on the democratic process in the classroom – to what degree and in what way students are able, by applying their own experiences and premises, to participate in the teaching process and consequently influence the structure of the lessons (this was referred to earlier as participation in decision-making).

We shall now address the question of how to incorporate the aims of democracy into environmental education i.e. that students develop into well informed members of society who are able to take an active part in environmental debates and also that environmental lessons remain characterised by participation. The fulfilment of these goals is dependent on the way in which we choose to present the environmental- and development issues in lessons. How we present these issues has a direct effect on the approach offered to the students, in terms of who has the right to make decisions in society as well as on the aspect of participation in the classroom.

Democracy in the Traditions of Environmental Education

In the following we will illustrate how fact-based environmental education, normative environmental education and education for sustainable development address the two democratic aims stated below:

- teaching is based on participation in decision-making ,
- students develop into well informed members of society who take an active role in social debates on the environment and sustainable development.

Participation in the classroom is sometimes restricted to lesson planning i.e. students are included in decisions about how different stages of a lesson are structured. Here we will address another aspect of participation, namely situations where students are given the opportunity of taking part in the teaching as they feel it should be carried out. A factor influencing this area of participation is the delegation of authority in the classroom. Here, authority refers to who has the right to speak during a lesson and who is simply regarded as a listener. The second democratic goal is also a matter of speakers and listeners. If the intention is that students are to take active roles in social debates, in their capacity of citizens, it is logical that they are permitted to learn about the various roles a citizen might have in such a debate. Both these aspects of the goals of democracy are directly associated with how environmental- and developmental problems are approached and dealt with during lessons.

Fact-based Environmental Education

In the fact-based approach to environmental education, environmental problems are seen as being caused by a lack of knowledge and information. This shortage can depend on two points; either people are not receiving enough information or that society itself lacks the knowledge and necessary skills to deal with the matter. In order to eliminate environmental problems, the solution to the first point would be in the form of information campaigns and/or educating people. The introduction of research projects would be a reasonable solution to the second point. According to this tradition, access to objective (irrefutable) knowledge would make it possible to deal with any environmental problems without involving any issues of values or ideology. The people who can supply this type of 'real' knowledge are scientists, or more specifically, natural scientists. It requires experts in the necessary fields of science to resolve environmental problems in accordance with this method of approach, which is characterised by having no moral standpoints: it is these experts that have the right to define what an environmental problem is and suggest the correct course of action required to solve it. This approach indicates a specific social order: experts define and instruct and the general public are informed. From a democratic perspective, this state of affairs would be defined as a meritocracy – a democratic system run by experts.

By identifying 'real' knowledge as a guideline for how we should relate to the natural world and social development, we also identify who has the right to speak about any related topics in classrooms i.e. those who have access to 'real' knowledge. Access is relative; this implies that the person who has access to a large amount of 'real' knowledge has more authority to comment on which environmentally moral standpoints are acceptable than a person who has restricted access. In a situation like this it is the teacher and those students who are able to quickly assimilate 'real' knowledge who are accredited with positions of authority in the classroom. This puts limitations on students' rights to discuss and present their own opinions and ideas, as it is the teacher who is automatically appointed as 'the one who knows best'. These restrictions affect students differently depending on their ability to assimilate 'real' knowledge.

Normative Environmental Education

The normative approach to environmental education presents environmental- and development problems as a question of attitudes, and aims to encourage students to adopt a specific standpoint (attitude) to these problems. When environmental- and developmental problems are regarded as attitude problems, and when the correct norm is regarded as being clear, there is the risk that discussions which explore alternative options can be regarded as being superfluous. This approach shares certain characteristics with indoctrination: e.g. if we were merely satisfied with the fact that people adopted an environmentally friendly attitude and began to dispose of food on compost heaps, recycle paper, glass, plastic etc. and buy environmentally friendly products, this would demonstrate a closer resemblance to indoctrination than to education.

In principle, this is what is achieved when we try to teach certain behavioural patterns to students – correct environmental behaviour – without first giving them the opportunity to understand and discuss the motives and premises that lie behind these actions. In order to legitimise these acts for students, teachers usually refer to international conventions, parliamentary decisions and target assessments in official documents.

In the case of participation in the classroom, the teacher (as with the fact-based approach) adopts the role as 'the one who knows best'. They are the ones who know the details of conventions and government decisions and are therefore also aware of which values are necessary to adopt. However, the distribution of authority between students is far from clear. Here the ability to absorb academic knowledge is not a crucial matter; it is, in all probability, each individual's measure of the 'correct' environmental commitment that is in focus. Another problem with this type of educational approach is that it can lead to a very specific understanding of citizens' role in society: they are the ones who obey the rules laid down by politicians or other people in positions of power. Here people in positions of authority have carte blanche in the matter of what are considered to be acceptable/unacceptable attitudes. This is, of course, not in line with democratic systems. A democracy allows each individual, on the basis of knowledge, experience and values, to form their own understandings and develop a line of reasoning to support their convictions.

Education for Sustainable Development

Pluralism is a keyword in education for sustainable development (ESD). This implies that the opinions and impressions of students can be expressed in the classroom. Pluralism also allows for a number of different perspectives and opinions on the issues treated in education to be discussed and studied. None of these perspectives are privileged beforehand in education. It is in the discussions that take place in the classroom where the different perspectives and opinions, and their implications are critically reviewed and valued. Teachers have a participatory role in the lessons; it is their responsibility to clarify, question, problematise and make suggestions in order to stimulate further discussions. Another central aspect of this educational approach is to discuss and formulate suitable methods of producing reference points that can be applied in the selection of knowledge and experience that make up lesson materials. Here it is important not to use a predetermined benchmark; each member of the group must make independent decisions and be encouraged to support them in the following discussions. Another important aspect is gaining experience from listening and participating in situations where others have different opinions. This educational approach functions in two ways, firstly, preparing students to take part in a democratic society in the future and secondly, that the school benefits from allowing environmental and developmental issues to be discussed in a democratic arena. From this perspective it is important that lessons include e.g. panel debates or role-playing activities which reflect real conflicts in society as well as students being permitted to participate in the environmental aspects of the organisation of the school.

Conclusion: Democracy Before, After or During Lessons

In summarising the above discussions, it is possible to say that the three traditions of environmental education represent three different ways of regarding the role of democracy in education. The aim of fact-based environmental education is to provide objective facts as a basis for opinion-making; in Normative environmental education to coordinate public will with political consensus, and in ESD to provide an arena for democratic communication and justification. The different democratic perspectives also imply that there is a difference in the view on where the democratic process takes place. In the Fact-based tradition, the democratic process comes *after* education – education is the task of preparing the students for their participation in a democratic society by providing them with essential knowledge. In the Normative tradition, the democratic process comes *before* education – the political debate on the values and knowledge that future development should rest on, and consequently what should be taught in school, comes first. Finally, in ESD the democratic process is an integral part of the education process and is situated *in* education – the critical discussion on different alternatives and their implications is an essential part of education itself.

Thus the conclusion suggested here is that ESD provides better conditions for the fulfilment of the democratic aims of schools than the other traditions of environmental education.

rning of Knowledge and
rals

In chapter eight we noted that education philosophy was a crucial factor in teaching on the environment and sustainable development. A central aspect in all pedagogical philosophies is the teaching approach. In order to be able to make fruitful decisions about lesson content and teaching methods, it is important to acquire an understanding of the learning process. Knowledge of the learning process is therefore a central aspect in the development of competence with education for sustainable development.

This chapter begins with a presentation of how learning morals and knowledge can be understood. This will be followed by an illustration of how learning of knowledge also involves a learning of viewpoints, which are important components in how individuals see the world or life as a whole. A consequence of this connection is that the usual division that exists between learning knowledge and learning morals is cast aside, which highlights a different approach to the teaching process. In this chapter we will use the learning processes within the natural science subjects as an illustration.

The Learning Process

Learning and Experience

One way of describing learning is to see it as a process of creating a relationship between what we already know and the new material being presented. For example, if we know what an apple looks like and then see a pear, we attempt to identify the pear by comparing it to the apple. It is these comparisons that create the relationship between what we already know and the new object. Comparisons are generally made by creating differences and similarities between that which we already know and that which is new to us. In the case of the apple and the pear, there are a number of differences and similarities; it is in the creation of these that we expand our range of experience. That which we already know is immediately understandable, and that which is immediately understandable is what we understand as being 'real'. If something is immediately understandable to us, we can say that it 'stands fast'.[1] Those people who understand atomic theory see the atoms as being immediately understandable, whilst those who have little knowledge of the subject regard anything to do with atoms as being highly unreal and abstract. Our understanding of reality develops at the same pace as our expansion of what stands fast.

Learning can therefore be described as the process of creating differences and similarities in relation to what stands fast for an individual.

If there is too great a distance between that which stands fast and the new material, learning cannot take place; we are unable to form relevant differences and similarities. One explanation of the learning problems arising in schools today is that there is a gap between the knowledge of daily life that the students posses and the scientific knowledge that they are expected to learn. If the students are not given sufficient help this causes difficulties in the learning process.

Learning Takes Place in Encounters with the Surrounding World

Encounters with the surrounding world present us with learning opportunities that enable us to form new differences and similarities. For example, in the case of learning about the natural world we can encounter nature in a variety of ways: books, films, conversations and by physically being in a natural environment. The encounters offered to students are often deciding factors in what

---

1   This expression comes from the work of the Austrian philosopher Ludwig Wittgenstein (1969/1992). In Wickman & Östman (2001, 2002a, b) this learning perspective is described further.

they learn. If we ask two groups of students about the direction of flow in a number of rivers and one group (A) has access to an ordinary map and the other group (B) to a relief map, it is very likely that we will receive different answers from the groups. Group A might say that the rivers flow downwards and group B will probably say that the water flows from higher ground to lower ground. The reason for the different answers is that the encounters involved in the two different teaching aids facilitate two separate ways of forming differences and similarities[2]. Our meaning making and our learning are thus not only dependent on what stands fast, but also on the encounters that we create for ourselves or are presented with. Accordingly, selecting the encounters that are to be presented to the students is an important aspect of lesson planning; this selection needs to accommodate what the students already know in addition to the intended objectives of the lesson.

Learning Morals

As ethics is a central part of ESD, we will mention a number of aspects involved in the process of learning morals and later apply these to illustrate that learning of morals can be understood in the same way as the learning of knowledge.

Learning to Make and Apply Moral Judgements

Learning morals involves learning how to make absolute value judgements. We can illustrate this by examining a recording from a lesson. During the lesson, in which students had been given the task of discussing the pros and cons of nuclear power, two different types of opinion were expressed. Lisa says that nuclear power is good because it is cheap. This is an example of a relative opinion i.e. the opinion is made in relation to a specific objective: we all would prefer cheaper energy. In this instance, nuclear power is allocated

---

2   See further Schoultz, Säljö & Wyndham (2002).

relative value. Emma opposes this opinion – 'but nuclear power is not good for the environment'. In this case the environment is given absolute value, which implies that the environment is something we should not damage. Emma has made a moral judgement since she feels that the environment is something that we always ought to respect. As a result of Emma's statement, in the ensuing, lively debate the rest of the group underwent a shift from making relative judgements to making moral judgements, that is absolute value judgements.

It is by participating in this type of activity that we learn how to make moral judgements. In the above situation it was a case of learning how to make moral instead of relative judgements.

In the above exercise, students also learnt that it is both valid and relevant to discuss energy consumption in environmental moral terms. Learning morals also encompasses the need to learn when morals are at risk, i.e. when it is suitable or necessary to make a moral judgement. If we visited a school at the beginning of the 20th Century, students would most probably not have learnt that environmentally moral discussions on the topic of energy consumption were both valid and relevant. This observation would support the fact that the relevancy of moral judgements (absolute value judgements) varies throughout history and even between cultures.

Knowing whether or not to make a moral judgement is also related to specific situations. E.g. if we see a person killing a bee, we might confront him/her with a moral statement; however if the person responded by saying that they had allergic reactions to bee stings we would probably retract the statement.

By experiencing this type of event, a person can learn to distinguish between situations where moral judgements are either appropriate or inappropriate.

Learning Norms

Learning morals includes learning a specific conception of the right and most desirable way of relating to and behaving towards humans and nature. If, for example, on a field trip one student (A) hits another (B) or disturbs a bird's nest and the teacher intervenes by saying that the act was wrong – 'Don't do that!' – this statement is a way for the teacher to communicate what is worth striving for in life: what is the correct or incorrect action. The teacher's correction is not simply a matter of stating that it is wrong to hit (B) or to disturb that particular bird's nest; but is rather an indication that it is wrong to hit people and harm animals. Here the teacher tries to teach correct behaviour: a specific way of relating to humans and animals in general. This way of teaching morals is, to a large extent, about getting people to learn norms regarding the right and wrong ways of treating people and nature. We can term this specific form of learning morals as learning of norms.

Learning to Distinguish Between Norms and Moral Commitments

We learn a large number of norms in our lives and these norms often stand in contrast to each other. If we are boxers we learn about different ways of hitting other people, whereas in school we are taught that it is wrong to hit people. Norms are often associated with specific practices. Some people are completely against boxing; this is due to the fact that they have a specific moral commitment. It is possible to distinguish between following a norm and having a commitment: a commitment is a belief in a value which is applicable in all aspects of life. Learning a norm, therefore, does not mean that one takes on a commitment: one can learn that something is right yet maintain a certain distance from it. It is also possible to regard a commitment as something personal and that which characterises an individual, whilst a norm belongs to the 'social' and characterises a social activity.

Is it possible, then, to determine whether or not a person has a commitment or *if* they are merely playing along i.e. following the norm. In our daily lives we have ways of determining the difference when we are unsure. This is illustrated in the following exchange between two students.

Peter: I think it is wrong to exploit the natural environment.
Adam: What do you mean by that?
Peter: I mean that using nature for our own ....

Adam: Do you really mean that?
Peter: Yes I believe it's wrong.
Adam: But what shall we eat then?

Peter's response to Adam's first question is to attempt to explain what he meant. However, Adam did not require any further clarification, but instead wanted to be sure that Peter really believed in what he was saying, i.e. he asked the question to be certain that what Peter said was a commitment. In order to be sure of this he reworded his first question, which resulted in Peter being able to tell Adam what he wanted to know. Following that it was possible to start a discussion on the topic of whether or not it is reasonable to have such a commitment.

It is by participating in or observing these types of conversations that we learn the differences between following a norm and believing in something and how to make those differences clear during communication.

Learning Morals via Ways of Encountering

There is a great difference between being approached as a person or as a member of a group. As a person one is unique, but as a member of a group one is a part of a social community. As a group member, the norms governing the situation or culture in which the encounter takes place are important: one is approached according to predetermined conceptions and norms. When a person is approached as an individual, he or she has a value regardless of their possession of specific characteristics and knowledge. The individual is approached with an open attitude; there are no preconceived notions or instrumental desires in the encounter. In this way of encountering an individual, the individual already has a value. Here we can discuss the moral dimension in terms of the manner of encountering.

Similarly we can encounter nature in different ways. When nature constitutes a source for learning of specific knowledge, we can refer to the encounter as closed. In closed encounters, nature is allocated instrumental value. It has a specific purpose, namely to learn knowledge. To clarify this reasoning, we can say that students are going to classify insects or minerals by going out and collecting insects and killing them or hammer mineral samples out of larger rocks. Their actions are based on the idea that they shall learn something and the insects and the minerals are the means for acquiring this goal.

In other cases we might encounter nature without having any such ambitions and intentions or any preconceived notions about the encounter. We can regard this way of encountering nature as open. In this approach towards the natural world it already has its own value.

Learning Ethical Reflection

In order to reflect ethically it is necessary to learn the various moral aspects which have been discussed above, since ethics are a matter of reflecting on morals by applying reason. This reflection can be a matter of critically comparing alternative norms and convictions. It can also be a case of critically evaluating the various alternatives. To enable such a comparative evaluation, we must first have access to a form of benchmark (see chapter five). For example, anthropocentric ethics have human beings as a benchmark; this implies that anything that is good for human beings is considered good. These benchmarks can also be critically reviewed.

The Learning Process

The process of moral learning can be compared with the process of learning knowledge. In an encounter , individuals can sometimes immediately create a relationship to what stands fast, whereas at other times they cannot. When they cannot it often becomes apparent in their actions; they ask a question, they hesitate, etc. On these occasions – which can occur, for example, when a person is not familiar with how to use a concept or a word or when he/she does not know what kind of moral situation is involved in an encounter – the person has to stage a new encounter – with the teacher, the textbook, a friend, a computer, etc, – in order to continue the practice with which they are involved. They can, of course, also reflect in order to find new ways of creating a relationship to what stand fast for them.

Thus learning, both cognitive and moral, always involves the prior experiences of individuals. When the prior experiences are successfully related to what the individual experiences in the learning situation, learning has taken place. Therefore the establishment of new relations means that earlier experiences take on a new or extended significance and, as a consequence, the individual is able to act in a new or modified way in future situations.

At the same time learning is situated, since it is in the encounter that learning takes place. When individuals learn it is always in relation to what other people say and do in the current situation, i.e. they respond to, take up points, argue against, agree with etc. other participants in the conversation. Furthermore, it is done in relation to the activity the individuals participate in.

Learning Knowledge and Values Simultaneously

Schools are institutions within society which have the function of teaching the younger generation values and attitudes. This means that students are not only expected to learn the scientific meanings (concepts, principles, theories etc.), but also to develop viewpoints on the sciences, people, nature and the relationship between people and nature.

In curricula, syllabi and textbooks there is often a differentiation between learning knowledge and learning attitudes and values. They are regarded as being two separate processes in both space and time. In curricula and syllabi, it is normal to distinguish between learning objectives i.e. knowledge, concepts, skills, etc. and social objectives i.e. attitudes, points of view, values, etc. Textbooks are often formed by the principle of necessary facts first and practical application second, and only then investigating value questions such as environmental or health issues.

By discussing what is actually involved in the process of learning knowledge, we shall attempt to illustrate that when we learn knowledge we simultaneously learn specific ways of viewing and that these ways of viewing constitute important aspects of our worldview. This implies that the differentiation commonly made between learning knowledge and learning values and attitudes is not reasonable.

Knowledge – Worldview

Certain basic criteria for how the natural world should be studied and depicted within the natural sciences were introduced as early as 17th and 18th Centuries.[3] Possibly the most radical aspect was that nature should be examined and approached as if it were a material object. Nature was not to be considered as something that possessed morals or values – neither in itself nor in relation to humans. Anybody wanting to create knowledge about nature had to do so by examining and describing nature in terms of material states and objects.

This approach towards the natural world is linked to certain objectives held by the community of the natural sciences. The purpose of these objectives is to allow for the formulation of general truths, which in turn enable scientists to explain and predict all the processes that take place in the natural world. It is important to note, however, that a large number of other organisations and communities with other objectives have different demands on what constitutes an acceptable approach to describing and investigating the natural world.

The difficulties that people often experiences when learning science can be due to the fact that it requires the usage of totally different communication criteria than we are used to in our daily lives.[4]

In order to facilitate the learning process, it is therefore important that any teaching begins from the students' understanding, i.e. the teaching must begin in what stands fast for them. Allowing the students to practice the new criteria will broaden the scope of what stands fast for them. A lot of time must be allowed for this process

---

3   von Wright (1989) and Toulmin (1990) give an accessible and informative depiction of how scientific knowledge of nature is connected to a specific view of nature.
4   See Östman (1996, 1998).

and teaching new theories and concepts should therefore take place in stages.

Learning scientific knowledge about the natural world thus involves that we learn to follow a number of criteria about how we should interpret nature. We have already touched upon one of these criteria. There are several other criteria that have the same function in scientific language. When these criteria are put together to create a logical, coherent system within e.g. a subject, they form what we can refer to as a worldview.[5]

Individual knowledge is, therefore, part of a much larger picture – a worldview – which is based on a number of criteria. Varying worldviews differ because they create different ways of seeing the world: they convey different descriptions of the world.[6] Each description makes up, so to speak, a perspective of the world. If we learn specific scientific knowledge we must simultaneously learn how to apply the criteria of which the knowledge is a part. One can therefore claim that knowledge is indivisible; we must accept the whole 'package' or worldview, in order to gain access to individual knowledge.

We have addressed one of the many different criteria within scientific knowledge production. This specific criterion touches upon what is usually referred to as a view of nature: Regarding nature as material object represents a specific view of nature. These criteria, or for that matter worldviews, are learned at the same time as we learn knowledge. To further clarify this state of contemporaneousness, the term companion meaning can be used: learning scientific meaning (the meaning of scientific words) is followed by other meanings e.g. a view of the natural world.[7]

5   The American philosopher Stephen Pepper (1942) claims that in principle there are seven different hypotheses or world views concerning the matter of how we understand the fundamental characteristics of the natural world, how reliable knowledge can be assimilated and what constitutes evidence for the existence of an object. See Kilbourn (1998) for an example of the seven hypotheses depicted in an educational context.

6   In one way the concept 'hypothesis' is more suitable than 'worldview' since the detailed criteria are hypotheses rather than complete and thoroughly proved descriptions of the world.

7   This term was introduced by Roberts & Östman (1998) and is clearly illustrated in their book about the importance of bringing attention to companion meanings in education.

Companion Meanings and Moral Debate

It is important to be aware of companion meanings in the learning process since they can sometimes be at the centre of moral debate. During the 19th Century, the natural sciences were exposed to a great deal of criticism because, in the eyes of the critics, they interpreted the natural world as an object or a means of achieving human ends. During the latter half of the 20th Century, eco feminism has raised similar criticism. Gender debates are often based on attention being brought to companion meanings within various activities or sectors.

It is, therefore, reasonable that ethical reflection encompasses the critical study of companion meanings within various practices. The significance of worldviews for moral norms and convictions can equally be brought into critical focus.

Further Reading

The learning approach presented in this chapter can be called sociocultural. The following books give a comprehensive account on sociocultural perspectives on learning:

Chaiklin, Seth, & Lave, Jean (Eds.). (1996). *Understanding practice. Perspectives on activity and context*. Cambridge: Cambridge University Press.

Wells, Gordon. (1999). *Dialogic Inquiry: Toward a Sociocultural Practice and Theory of Education*. Cambridge: Cambridge University Press.

Wertsch, James (1998). *Mind as Action*. Oxford: Oxford University Press.

Wertsch, James Del Rio, Pablo & Alvarez, Amelia (1995). *Sociocultural Studies of Mind*. Cambridge: Cambridge University Press.

Other Reference Literature

Kilbourn, Brent (1988). Root metaphors and education. In *Douglas Roberts & Leif Östman* (Eds.), pp. 25–38.

Östman, Leif (1996). Discourses, discursive meanings and socialization in chemistry education. *Journal of Curriculum Studies*, Vol. 28, pp. 37–55.

Östman, Leif (1998). How companion meanings are expressed by science education discourse. In *Douglas Roberts & Leif Östman* (Eds.), pp. 54–70.

Pepper, Stephen (1942). *World Hypotheses*. London: University of California Press.

Roberts, Douglas & Östman, Leif (Eds.) (1998). *Problems of Meaning in Science Curriculum*. London: Teachers College Press.

Schoultz, Jan; Säljö, Roger & Wyndham, Jan (2002). Heavenly talk. Discourse, artifacts, and children's understanding of elementary astronomy. *Human Development*, Vol 44, pp. 103–118.

Toulmin, Stephen (1990). *Cosmopolis. The Hidden Agenda of Modernity*. New York: Free Press.

Wickman, Per-Olof & Östman, Leif (2001). University Students During Practical Work: Can we make the learning process intelligible? In Helga Behrendt; Helmut Dahncke; Reinders Duit; Wolfgang Gräber; Michael Komorek; Angela Kross & Priit Reiska (Eds.), *Research in Science Education – past, present and future*. Dordrecht: Kluwer, pp. 319–324.

Wickman, Per-Olof & Östman, Leif (2002a). Learning as discourse change: A sociocultural mechanism. *Science Education*, Vol. 86, pp. 601–623.

Wickman, Per-Olof & Östman, Leif (2002b). Induction as an empirical problem: How students generalisze during practical work. *International Journal of Science Education*, Vol. 24, pp. 465–486.

Wittgenstein, Ludwig (1969/72). *Über gewissheit /On certainty*. New York: Harper & Row, Publishers.

von Wright , George Henrik (1986). *Science, Reason and Value*. Documenta 49. Stockholm: The Royal Swedish Academy of Sciences Information Department.

11 Teaching Sustainable Development

What are the Implications of Teaching Sustainable Development?

Based on the comparisons between Education for sustainable development and the other traditions of environmental education made in chapters eight and nine, and in addition to the perspectives on learning knowledge and morals that were discussed in chapter ten, we will, in this chapter, present a deeper study on the significance of teaching sustainable development. This will be done from a teaching perspective, i.e. we will take a closer look at the significance of the choices a teacher might make in the areas of goals, content and method. The question we are looking into here can be seen as: what are the implications of teaching sustainable development? The principles of education to be presented here are, however, not to be understood as predetermined guidelines for teaching sustainable development. The actual structure of this form of education must be based on locally based experience as well as the historical, social, cultural and geographical backgrounds which are part of each school. The principles will, therefore, represent possible reference points for continued reflection and discussion in the practice of education for sustainable development.

The Concept 'Sustainable Development'

To be able to discuss what it actually means to teach sustainable development, it is necessary to first make clear what the term actually means and how it stands in relation to education. But as was illustrated in chapter two, in any discussion it soon becomes apparent that there is no straightforward answer. A certain amount of guidance can be taken from the central international policies that have been formed on sustainable development. One of the first appearances of the term is in the Brundtland Report, in which sustainable development was defined as being:

> development that meets the needs of the present without compromising the ability of future generations to meet their own needs (World Commission on Environment and Development, 1987, p. 43).

In the plans of action which resulted from the international conference on the environment in Rio 1992, Agenda 21 states that sustainable development requires a cooperated plan of development between the three areas of environment, society and economy, and additionally that:

> Education is critical for promoting sustainable development and improving the capacity of the people to address environment and development issues . . . . It is critical for achieving environmental and ethical awareness, values and attitudes, skills and behaviour consistent with sustainable development and for effective public participation in decision-making (UNCED, 1992, chap. 36, p. 2).

The Baltic 21E proposal, the plan of action for education on sustainable development, which was adopted by education ministers from 12 countries in the Baltic region, contains several useful guidelines which illustrate what a 'sustainable' perspective might be in education. For example:

- sustainable development is a fundamental part of a healthy democracy and active citizenship,
- sustainable development is named as one of the main goals of the entire education system,
- sustainable development is to be integrated into existing subjects and the relationship between the natural sciences and social sciences needs to be strengthened,
- education for sustainable development is to address topics which will give insight into the global, regional and local aspects of sustainable development,
- the ethical dimension is central to understanding sustainable development,

192   © The Authors and Studentlitteratur

- education for sustainable development involves discussions and critical reviews of different alternatives and their consequences,
- the economical, social and environmental areas must be coordinated in such a way they are mutually beneficial to each other.

In chapter 8 it was said that the transition from environmental protection to sustainable development implies a broader perspective on the issues surrounding the subject. The points mentioned above are also an indication of this trend. This applies to aspects of time and space as well as content. From the time perspective, it implies that not only current environmental problems are studied, but also that attention is brought to the consequences of our present day activities on the right of future generations to enjoy the same quality of life. From a space perspective, it is about ensuring that the entire range of issues is approached from both a local and global point of view. Content refers to the fact that all sectors of society will be involved. Therefore this is not solely a matter of developing sustainable methods of utilising nature's resources but also includes creating a society which is socially and economically sustainable. Not least it concerns coordinating ecological, economical and social sustainability.

In brief it is about creating a 'good' society and consequently the optimum conditions for good health and a good standard of living. Sustainable development, therefore, touches on the whole of our environment and the kind of future society we would like to live in, as well as the necessary requirements for ensuring a good life for the coming generations.

It is easy to see that any concept that encompasses the 'good' life and the 'good' society will inevitably be the cause of many conflicts of interests and values. Even though science can supply us with a more or less uniform picture of environmental- and developmental problems, it is still up to individuals and groups in society to make their own interpretations and evaluations of the consequences of these problems in relation to the other activities they are involved in and consider important.

Accordingly, there is no general consensus on the interpretation of the concept of sustainable development. There are representatives from the entire political spectrum, which is a strong indicator of how little agreement there can be. There are those of the opinion that it is possible to create conditions for sustainable development within the framework of today's society, i.e. a liberally oriented and growth-based market economy. The contrasting opinion claims that sustainable development requires radical changes both in terms of the values and consumption habits of people as well as in global resource distribution.

The scientific community is equally unable to present an unequivocal picture of any problems presented by the implementation of sustainable development (see chapter 4). This allows for representatives outside the scientific community to present us with alternative interpretations of the state of the world and the opportunities that lie before us.

The fact that the sustainable development perspective allows for many different standpoints to be heard implies that it has a clearly ethical aspect where differing ideas of values, caring and responsibility are polarised. One such ethical question is; to who do the guidelines introduced by sustainable development policies actually apply, i.e. to whom do we have a responsibility when we make decisions or act? In chapter five there is a discussion of the different standpoints on the degree of consideration we could take on the following:

- the development opportunities for people all over the world,
- the quality of life for future generations,
- the well-being of organisms,
- the survival of all species and ecosystems.

The way in which we approach this range of different opinions is of crucial importance when formulating what type of guidelines are possible to introduce for sustainable development. Being able to effectively organise the broad range of differing values and interests so that each is given equal attention is indeed a great challenge for democratic societies. The diversity of opinions indicates that sustainable development cannot be restricted by a permanent definition; the concept itself should always be open to discussion. If this were achieved, sustainable development would share certain characteristics with the concept of democracy, as an ongoing dialogue which allow sustainable development to remain meaningful as opposed to being limited by a permanent definition. It is possible to see sustainable development functioning as a compass in the development of society: it can point in certain directions but gives neither information as to what will be encountered on the way nor of any predetermined destinations.

One of the main conclusions we have drawn is the fact that democracy should be an integral part of education. This implies that education must be pluralistic, i.e. it should reflect the diversity of understandings and opinions which are represented in the debate on questions relating to sustainable development. A main theme in this chapter is, therefore, the discussion on how democratic perspectives influence the decisions that affect teaching sustainable development, especially in terms of the goals, content and teaching methods.

An Educational Perspective

Here we will address the question of how particular aspects of a subject are dealt with in the actual practice of teaching. From a teacher perspective, this includes all the various choices available during a lesson. Research on the subject shows that a large proportion of a teacher's working day consists of situations where decisions have to be made. These situations are categorised into two principally different types: the type of situation that can arise spontaneously in the classroom and presents the question *how shall I deal with this?* This question demands an immediate answer and the teacher must rely on his/her previous experience in this situation. The other arises in the lesson planning stage and is of the type, *what are my alternatives?* Here there is time for reflection on the alternatives that are available, as well as the opportunity to evaluate possible outcomes of the chosen alternatives. Contrary to the first type of situation which mainly relies on experience, theoretical knowledge can be used as guidance. The following discussion in this chapter will be confined to the second type of question – the alternatives.

A basic division can be made between a choice of *purpose* and *goals*, a choice of *content*, and a choice of *teaching method*. In the following text we will address some principles within education when making decisions in teaching for sustainable development. A recurring theme in this discussion is that democratic thought is always central to teaching on the subject of sustainable development.

Selecting Goals and Motivating Factors in Teaching for Sustainable Development

How does one select goals and motivation in education particularly in such a diverse and unfixed area as sustainable development?

In the previous chapter we stated that there is an inherent democratic dilemma in the idea that education should encourage and advocate sustainable social development. Therefore, in the process of formulating the motives and goals for this type of education two problems are encountered. Firstly, sustainable development encompasses very complex problems, where a great many different standpoints exist: what kind of social development is actually supposed to be supported? Secondly, education systems often have clear democratic guidelines which stipulate that education is to support the principle of freedom to form one's own opinions. With this in mind, is it then possible to recommend a specific type of social development in school education?

It would seem therefore both unreasonable and undemocratic if a school attempts to instil predetermined solutions to the problems highlighted by sustainable development. It would be more reasonable, and from a democratic perspective necessary, for schools to educate citizens who have the ability to deal with the problematic issues presented by sustainable development. It is then a matter of coping with the complexity and diversity surrounding sustainable development in a democratic way. This is partly a matter of managing all the decisions that an individual must make when faced with the enormous array of products, services, lifestyles and identities which today's society offers.

The main purposes of education for sustainable development could be formulated in such a way that students who participate in the lessons:

(1) are given an opportunity to orientate themselves among the different viewpoints,

(2) receive knowledge and ethical awareness to critically evaluate the various alternatives,

(3) develop the ability to act upon the standpoints which have been formed,

(4) are allowed to participate in activities which demonstrate that it is meaningful to be engaged in issues which involve sustainable development.

A comprehensive goal for education for sustainable development, based on the above points, can be formulated in the following way.

After completing the course, students will be able to critically evaluate different approaches as well as be motivated to actively participate in democratic debates on the sustainable development of society.

The actual meaning of 'active participation in democratic debates' is to be understood as all the choices, which we as active members of society make when we e.g. consume products, travel, and are involved in discussions in different situations such as in schools, at home, at work and during our free time.

Choosing and Utilizing the Content of Education for Sustainable Development

Even in the matter of lesson content, the democratic perspective in education for sustainable development is of great importance. The choices made in the selection of teaching contents can be divided into three stages: choice, organisation and approach.

Choice

As a schoolteacher, there is often cause for concern when new subject content surfaces in the existing sphere of education. There is the worry that even more material and/or information will be introduced into the already overloaded subject area in which one is teaching. Creating an entirely new subject is one option, although there is then the practical problem of including the new subject into the school timetable. There is, however, the option of introducing the idea of sustainable development, not as a new subject, but rather as an *integrated perspective* which is applied to the existing content in all subjects. The perspective 'sustainable development' can then be seen as a tool in the selection process, where both students and teachers are involved in choosing relevant lesson content. As it is impossible to include all our culture's knowledge and information on the world in education, the process of selection is naturally a fundamental aspect of teaching. By applying the perspective of sustainable development we are more able to put forward questions such as what type of knowledge and skills are necessary in order for us to make the important choices in life. In the light of sustainable development, certain aspects will stand out as being more important than others, i.e. it acts as a guide as to where the emphasis should lie and how we should approach the content.

An important principle for the choice of content is that depictions and facts should be obtained from numerous sources. This means also using alternative perspectives and understandings, including those held by minority groups.

Another important aspect is the need to address *real problems* during lessons; problems which are relevant to the students' lives and the society in which they live, and preferably problems that the group has some influence over or can affect in some way. The immediate environment and the local community represent an important starting point for teaching for sustainable development (this also includes students' working environment, i.e. the school and health). It is of equal importance that these questions are not reduced to just localised issues, but on the contrary are related to more comprehensive concerns of sustainable development e.g. historical, societal and global aspects. Here it is possible to see that

198

working with sustainable development is a case of putting things *into context*, where the different areas and levels are seen as integral parts of a whole.

Organisation

We have already mentioned that sustainable development can be seen as an integrated perspective – something which is present in all school subjects. As all schools are different with regard to size, economical situation etc., the lessons can accordingly be organised in several different ways. Teaching for sustainable development can be approached from both a single subject or from larger theme based sessions where several teachers from different subjects participate. However, the central idea remains that students are given plenty of opportunities to assimilate the new knowledge they have learnt. This can be approached by relating the new areas of study to ones which have been covered earlier, as well combining knowledge and experiences from different subjects. A well thought-out method of *sequencing, progression* and *association* between the content and themes in different subjects is, therefore, of great importance to teaching for sustainable development.

Approach

In chapter 10 we illustrated the fact that there are norms in all the understandings and depictions of the reality we perceive – and that in the teaching process certain ways of seeing the world are inevitably offered to the student. With this in mind, it seems important that teachers ask themselves which information/knowledge is to be prioritised. One basic position in pluralistic education is that no particular perspective should be prioritised, although more latitude is allowed for perspectives which are considered important in society e.g. the scientific perspective on environmental problems.

Another result of the connection between facts and norms is that a *critical standpoint* appears as being central in the approach towards the actual knowledge content of the lessons. It is a matter of making a critical evaluation based on which perspectives and which interests are supported by the lesson material, and our understanding of how we should solve the various problems which are presented. In this way, students are given a more conscious understanding as to how they form their own opinions.

With a starting point in sustainable development, the actual purpose of teaching is altered, as is the actual approach to knowledge. A central point in education for sustainable development is therefore that the learning of theoretical knowledge is not a goal in itself. It is rather a case of *knowledge/skills being selected based on the idea that they are fruitful for understanding what sustainable development implies in terms of consequences for the lifestyles of individuals and society in general.* Therefore it is important to integrate discussions of the implications or effects of whatever it is students have learnt into the teaching process. These discussions could be in the form of standpoints regarding the development of modern society, our responsibilities towards future generations, products that one should avoid etc.

Selecting Methods and Approaches in Education for Sustainable Development

Education for sustainable development is not characterised by any specific teaching methods. The methods are determined, among other things, by the experiences and backgrounds of the students taking part in the lessons. However, we do suggest two guiding principles in the choice of teaching methods. Firstly, the chosen method must be related to the actual aim of the education – contributing towards the students' development in their role as members of a democratic society who are capable of critical evaluation. Secondly, that the teaching method is approached with the understanding that the process of learning takes place in the encounter between the student and the teaching material.

Experiencing Democracy

The main objective of education for sustainable development is the development of students' levels of competence in the area of participating in democratic processes, but it is also necessary that they see democratic participation as a meaningful activity. Education for sustainable development is, therefore, not simply a matter of preparing students for life in a democracy but is more a case of ensuring that students can *experience democracy* during lessons in order to gain a level of practical familiarity with democratic processes. This approach is based on the understanding that students are already regarded as being members of a democratic society during the course of their education i.e. that students are equal participants in the teaching process. Seen from this viewpoint, education for sustainable development is an education in democracy rather than an education about democracy.

It is, therefore, important to pay particular attention to the actual teaching process in education for sustainable development, e.g. how classroom discussions are conducted and how they affect each student's understanding of their role as a democratic citizen. Questions such as: who has the right to speak; are there any restrictions when speaking; who, if anybody, is in possession of the correct answers; have a great deal of influence on how students come to value their own opinions (see chapter nine). Additionally, it is important that students learn to listen to, respect and take into consideration differing opinions.

The Encounter

In the teaching process there is usually either a focus on syllabus-based subjects or the needs and interests of the students. A way of avoiding this either/or approach is to take the encounter between the students and the lesson material as a starting point (see chapter 11). It is in this encounter between student and the knowledge which our culture has accumulated throughout history that the learning process takes place.

By taking this encounter as a starting point in education for sustainable development, there is an effect on the roles of student and teacher during lessons. For the student it is a case of becoming an *active creator* in the lesson. A central aspect of the learning process is, however, that the student can make associations between previous and new experiences. If, in a new encounter, the concepts are too far removed from the student's previous experiences, nothing can hope to be gained. The knowledge or information would then fall into the category of instrumental learning, which lacks relevance to the student's life. The teacher's role can be seen as a supervisor in the encounter – someone who creates situations, clarifies the purpose of an activity, asks questions to stimulate discussions or ideas and participates in the evaluation process of what has been learnt.

The encounters in education can be seen as being different in character. Hence the teacher must reflect on how the correct balance can be created between *direct* and *indirect* encounters and *open* and *closed* encounters respectively.

Indirect encounters involve an encounter with the surrounding environment in the form of texts, lessons/lectures, images etc. The advantage of indirect encounters is that students have access to knowledge, which is part of our cultural archive, as well as access to parts of the world or experiences which are not practically possible to experience at first hand. The disadvantage lies in the fact that students only receive access to somebody else's version of whatever the topic is, as well as the fact that out of necessity the version has to be a simplification of reality.

A *direct encounter* involves the subject matter being studied at first hand; by using sight, touch, smell etc. and experiencing the encounter wherever it occurs naturally. This quite clearly increases the possibilities for students to form their own understanding of what is being studied. It can also be assumed that there will be an increased likelihood that students develop an emotional association with the object of study. For example, a first hand encounter with 'nature' compared with the same encounter in a text book can therefore be important to the type of relationship created, and consequently for the individual's future attitude towards the natural world.

A *closed encounter* implies that the encounter as a predetermined objective; the encounter should result in students assimilating certain specifically selected knowledge. The encounter is a means of

202

achieving the objective. This type of encounter can be used to transfer certain skills and information to students which are regarded as being important in the make up of a democratic citizen. The student therefore becomes a recipient of knowledge which others have decided is necessary in the process of education.

In an *open encounter*, the encounter has value in itself and it is entirely open as to what students learn. This type is not only a people to people encounter, but can also involve e.g. the natural environment. Here the student becomes an active and responsible creator of his/her experience; there is more of a striving towards a certain level of quality in the received knowledge rather than concentrating on learning predetermined facts. In the discussions that take place during an open encounter, all students have equal status when exchanging views and opinions of their respective experiences. An open encounter can take the form of, for example, a field trip to a location which has suffered some environmental damage, with follow up discussions on the value of nature or global resource distribution.

Conclusion

From a teaching/learning perspective, the characteristics of education for sustainable development which have been presented can be summarised in the following way:

- a primary objective of students gaining the ability to actively participate in democratic processes and having the desire to do so,
- the democratic process is to be an integral part of the education which students can experience first hand,
- the student has an active and responsible role in the creation of his/her own educational progress,
- the teacher's role is that of a supervisor or instructor,
- during the lessons there is an attempt to achieve a balance between direct – indirect and open – closed encounters respectively,
- this approach to education assumes that there are many ways of describing, evaluating and relating to a problem and its solu-

tions, and also acknowledges a conflict of interests between these perspectives,

- when lesson content/material is being selected, many different sources are used to ensure that students are exposed to a broad knowledge base from which to reflect and take standpoints,
- a critical approach is a central feature – this implies that the various interests behind each perspective and the implications of each course of action will be reviewed,
- sustainable development is seen as a perspective of consolidation that helps students and teachers to relate new knowledge/information to that which has been learnt previously, as well as linking knowledge and perspectives from different subjects,
- the topics included in lessons will include historical events and future consequences as well as local and global aspects,
- most aspects of the education will, to a great extent, begin with problems which students can relate to and be comfortable with and ultimately influence with their own actions.

Further Reading

Scott, William & Gough, Stephen (2003). *Sustainable Development and Learning: framing the issues*. London & New York: Routledge Falmer.

Scott, William & Gough, Stephen (2004). *Key Issues in Sustainable Development and Learning: a critical review*. London & New York: Routledge Falmer.

Sterling, Stephen (2001). *Sustainable Education: Re-visioning Learning and Change*. Foxhole, Dartington, Totnes, Devon: Green Books.

Other Reference Literature

UNCED (1992). *Agenda 21*. London: Regency Press.

World Commission on Environment and Development (1987). *Our Common Future*. Oxford: Oxford University Press.

Baltic 21E – An Agenda for Education in the Baltic Sea Region. Baltic 21, Series No 1/02. http://www.baltic21.org/?publications,21#67.

12 Teaching Models within Sustainable Development

In this chapter we will present three teaching models that were created within the framework of the project 'Sustainable Development in Schools'.[1] The objectives of the project were, via the interaction between research into environmental education and the practical teaching experience of education for sustainable development, to develop teaching models, which could later be applied in practical teaching situations. The project consisted of nine teams of teachers, all representing different subject areas, school types and geographical areas in Sweden. All the teachers attended a series of seminars where many of the areas appearing in this book were addressed. Time was also allocated in which teachers could exchange their own personal teaching experiences. Each of the teams received continuous support during the project work in their respective schools.

'The Shopping Bag' – A Student-active 'Anthropological' Project

The sustainable production of food is one of the most formidable challenges within sustainable development; it is also a chosen theme in environmental studies at an upper secondary school in Sweden. In the project, students follow the chain of production in reverse from the dinner table to the actual producers, i.e. the far-

1 The project was financed by the The Swedish National Agency for School Improvement and the results will be published during 2004. The description of the teaching models in this chapter is taken from the forthcoming publication. The project leaders were Johan Öhman and Leif Östman.

mers via supermarkets, wholesalers etc. According to the guidelines in the project, students research questions such as the elements that influence production, distribution, storage etc. as well as how each of these stages affects the environment. The team leaders of this particular project were two teachers within different subject areas (social studies and science respectively). The entire timeframe for the project was 50 clock hours.

Specific ESD Characteristics

- Students are given the opportunity to integrate issues concerning ecology, economy, politics and social development.
- With reference points in actual problems, the objective is to give general insights into situations which will have an influence on students' lives in the future.
- The project is primarily task oriented, therefore the focus of the project is on students developing a *certain quality of knowledge*: to understand rather than to memorise, to develop a high quality of reasoning rather than delivering the right answer.
- The project work is based on *direct encounters* with employees involved in the food industry; students also have the opportunity to actively participate in the areas of production concerning the project.
- The students are encouraged to be both active and responsible in their approach to their own development and that of fellow students. The teacher's role in the project is to offer guidance when necessary.

Teachers Presentation: Acquiring Knowledge Through Close Contact of The First Kind

The following is a summary of a teacher's account of the project work.

The initial stage of this project is a general introduction to the subject, which includes issues such as fertilizer emissions, species depletion, pesticides, agricultural and economic history, social

206

development, transportation etc. There are regular meetings where students report back to the group and present their work. An important feature of the project is that students learn to identify and understand the interests which influence the food industry. This is done by carrying out *case studies* which illustrate that, notwithstanding the high levels of skills and information within the industry, there are still many situations where problems occur.

The introduction is followed by the actual 'shopping bag' project – two bags of shopping are divided among groups of students. Prior to this the groups have already selected a category of food – cereal products (bread, pasta), fruit and vegetables, meat, and dairy products (including eggs). The first task is to prepare and eat the food – something that all the students enjoy.

The theoretical work begins with students deciding on a *plan of action*: which aspects of the environment should be addressed, making a contact list of people/organisations, making a list of sources for getting product information etc. Students are given some time to complete the plan before reporting back to the teachers who can advise or ask for further clarification etc. Students are given a checklist to facilitate the planning stage; the list includes different aspects and areas of research which either could or should be included in the project work.

On completion of the action plan, students then contact local supermarkets and convenience stores and try to find out if there are any problems relevant to the group's chosen products, e.g. fruit and vegetables. Thereafter the students follow the chain of production to the wholesalers, manufacturers and finally the producers/farmers.

In preparation for the final stage, arrangements have been made with farmers so that students can visit and participate in life on a farm for a 2–3 day period. These visits allow students first hand knowledge of how farmers see environmental issues, economics, agricultural policies etc. In addition, field trips to food production plants, dairies and slaughter houses/butchers are included in the project.

Compiling reports and other final details, additional questions etc., may require further input from the teachers. During the whole project, individual groups are gathered for guidance and discussion meetings every two to three weeks. It is also beneficial for all the groups to meet together, as this gives everybody an insight into the process as a whole, as well as groups having the opportunity to discuss and exchange ideas. As teachers, we regularly point out that this project will be graded by continuous assessment and not on a final test. Students are also required to keep a log of their activities, which may vary from group logs to individual logs; these are also to be handed in at the end of the project.

Conclusions drawn from the project work: It is important that the teachers concerned follow a well structured approach to the project, with a clear emphasis on what is expected from the students in each phase. Within this frame, students are given ample opportunity to select a particular focus and orientation for their chosen area of study. This approach lies within the framework for the model known as adaptive leadership: this is applied in situations where a lot of general information is given in the beginning and is successively replaced by group or individual feedback/guidance meetings in which students are given a lot of freedom. Students often require guidance in locating and identifying information – we can help in this area by referring students to information sources outside school, reference literature and the Internet. The teachers involved in the project feel that they have a good overview of what the students are learning due to the regular meetings and discussions, log books and final reports and presentations. We feel sure that this model can be extended to subject areas other than the food industry.

Sustainable Development in Social Science – the Conflict Perspective

In this upper secondary school, sustainable development has been the guiding principle for the selection of the content and work methods within the subject of social science. The main objective is to highlight the democratic perspectives in the lessons and ultimately allow for students to 'experience' democracy, i.e. they are given plenty of opportunities to express their experiences, opinions, values and needs. Increasing the democratic environment during lessons is achieved by allowing them to be involved in deciding which topics are to receive more focus, successively increasing independent work assignments and introducing work methods which allow for greater expression of students' individual theoretical knowledge and skills etc. The content is oriented towards enhancing pluralism, conflict perspectives, and students' rights to form their own opinions. An aim of this project is to demonstrate the possibilities of introducing sustainable development as a perspective that encompasses the entire teaching/learning process within a subject.

Specific ESD Characteristics

- The project emphasises the range of *different opinions* on areas such as welfare and the distribution and management of the resources available in society.
- A central aspect of the study is that students gain an understanding of the relationship between *individual* and *collective* opinions/ decisions, as well as the requirements and conflicts that can result.
- The conflicts surrounding sustainable development between various interest groups in society represent a central feature in the project.
- The economic dimensions within these conflicts are addressed, i.e. *economic growth versus sustainable development*.
- The conflicts are approached from a global perspective, with particular attention being given to the relationship between poverty and environmental issues.
- The *moral* and *democratic* characteristics of conflict are also included in the project.
- The issues that appear on the agenda for *public debate* are also included in the study, as are the attempts of various groups to receive attention in the media.

Teachers Presentation: Pluralism and Conflicts

The following is a summary of a teacher's presentation of the project work.

The project involves seven stages, although these need not necessarily be followed in the order presented here.

1. *The Media and forming public opinion*: This stage comprises a discussion on the power of the public agenda and who actually decides what a social problem is. This represents the basis towards an understanding of the problems of interest groups and efforts to bring 'their' issues to attention in the media. The assignment in this stage involves a simple empirical study of the issues dominating the news during a given time frame. The purpose of the assignment is to stimulate discussion about the values and interests that influence the media, in addition to providing an insight into the necessity of a public debate on our shared natural environment and sustainable development. This is followed up with a discussion on evaluating news reports and the priorities that influence the selected news items. This stage is accompanied by a study and discussion of the theoretical models relevant in media coverage, e.g. 'the communication model', 'gatekeepers' (mass media as a form of indirect communication) and the 'news values' model.

2. *The employment market*: This stage brings focus to the well-known conflicts which occur between employers and employees. Here we have chosen the issues of the work environment and sick leave as focus points. The aim of this assignment is to present examples of how conflicts of interest in the employment market are expressed, and to demonstrate how these stand in relation to how the same groups understand the idea of sustainable development. Here we concentrate on the increasing numbers of people off sick – as this most effectively reflects the issue of how we can best manage the available resources in society, which in this case is the work force, or 'human capital'. The issues that have been discussed include: Why is the increase in the number of sick absentees a problem? Whose best interests lie in the reduction of these figures? Do the various groups represented in the employment market have different opinions as to the causes of increased sick leave? What are the different suggestions of the various groups for solving this issue? What are the factors influencing the contrasting opinions held by the groups as to the solution of the problem?

3. *Society's economic resources and energy issues etc.*: This stage looks into the management of society's resources. It is introduced by an overview of different resource categories, and followed by a discussion on the various ways (and the opinions on them) that resources can be utilised without leading to open conflicts. The assignments which feature during this stage include a role play, which emphasises the differences between individual and collective rationality, a discussion on the possible interpretations of the term 'welfare', and an exercise which involves finding ways of securing the welfare for the future by applying knowledge of today's resource management and consumption habits.

4. *Politics (democracy, political ideas, forms of government)*: Here the focus is on practical approaches towards dealing with conflicts of interest on a public level. In the introductory discussion on democracy we have chosen to put forward the following questions:
   - What is the significance of democracy? How does it work? Is there an alternative?
   - What are the pros and cons of democracy?
   - Are there any values that should precede democracy? If this is the case, who is to decide on these matters?
   - Do we have a moral responsibility towards each other? Why/ Why not? Whose rights should be considered? Animals? Future generations?
   - What are the boundaries for our moral responsibility?

5. *Social economics*: In stage five there is an in depth analysis on the conflicting elements on economic growth versus sustainable development. Students discuss the potential of different economic systems in dealing with the environmental effects of production, as well as forming economic incentives which could lead to rational individual behaviour and would be collectively acceptable. This stage is a continuation of the line of reasoning which was introduced in the section on resource management.

6. *International relations*: Here the discussion is taken to a global level to address the role of international organisations in establishing better conditions for cooperation in environmental issues. We also emphasis the association between social issues,

e.g. the conflict of interests between poverty and environmental issues.

7. *Building a society*: The final task in the project sees the students creating their own society from scratch. The idea here is to pool all the experiences and information gathered in the previous stages: E.g. students must take standpoints on issues such as resource distribution and allocation, resolving conflicts between various parties, ensuring a sustainable future for society etc. This exercise is presented below.

Exercise:

After a thousand years of war, over population and environmental damage, the end of the world is a fact. You are included in a group of two thousand people who have managed to escape from planet Earth to the nearest inhabitable planet. You only managed to bring with you simple tools and almost no resources. The new planet is almost identical to Earth before humankind destroyed it, in that it has varying climates, a functioning eco system and a multitude of species.

There is no possibility of returning to Earth. The new planet must be colonised, but how should this be done without repeating the mistakes made on planet Earth? Your group receives the following task: A number of suggestions are to be presented before the assembly, where hopefully an agreement will be reached on how the survivors will successfully colonise the planet without causing history to repeat itself.

Questions to be answered in preparation for the presentation:

- How shall we organise ourselves? To ensure our survival we will require some sort of inventory of our resources.
- Will there be a need for political organisations?
- What is the best way of meeting the needs and wishes of all the people?
- How can criminality be avoided and what steps should be taken in the event of criminal activity?

- How are we to reach agreements on common laws and practices?
- How do we make sure all tasks are carried out? Is a reward system necessary?
- Will there be any right of ownership of the land or resources?
- How will schools/education and health care be organised?
- Will there be a requirement for any kind of defence policies?

The Conscious Consumer in a Sustainable Society – an All-encompassing Theme

In this example, our role as consumers in a sustainable society is the theme in a secondary school project. The main objective of the project is to allow students to strengthen their role as responsible citizens in terms of becoming conscious consumers in a sustainable society. The ambition is to develop knowledge of the consequences of our actions as consumers, as well as underlining the ethical connotations of the choices made.

The theme work involves the cooperation of two teachers (from the social sciences and natural sciences respectively) and spans a six-week period, which is a total of 30 clock hours of teaching. There have not been any strict divisions between the subjects; in certain cases both teachers have participated whilst in others one teacher has continued the lessons where the other left off. The written evaluation and the concluding role-play in which students demonstrate their new knowledge and skills are also common events.

The approach towards the content has been characterised by three perspectives. 1) An *environmental perspective* where students have the opportunity to take responsible action in their immediate environment, as well as forming a personal standpoint towards the overall concept of sustainable development. 2) An *International perspective* to enable the students to see their own environment from a global perspective, create a feeling of international solidarity, as well as preparing for a pluralistic society with close contacts which cross cultural and national borders. 3) An *ethical perspective* to establish and develop students' abilities to make individual standpoints which take the natural environment and the lives of others into consideration.

Specific ESD Characteristics

- There is a *progression* in the content which is related to the actions of each individual. It starts with the individual perspective, expands to the local and finishes in the global perspective.
- The lessons contain both *closed and open encounters*. The closed encounters involve students learning basic facts, concepts and models. However, these are continuously related to the theme of universal issues: an example is how the concept of energy is treated in order to facilitate students forming standpoints on the consumption of certain products. The open encounters mainly deal with the discussions of alternatives and viewpoints where individual students' standpoints are in focus.
- The *conflict perspective* is present in all aspects of the entire project: different alternatives available in approaching an issue, the varying interests behind each alternative, different ethical perspectives on questions which are addressed etc. The conflict perspective is related to both the individual – the internal conflicts experienced by people – and society: the conflicts among different groups of people around the world. The aim is to allow students to practice establishing standpoints in relation to these conflicts with the help of both scientific knowledge and ethical reasoning. In this way, both facts and morals relate to each other.
- The example illustrates how the content can be integrated *into two subjects*, in which the respective teachers can address different aspects of the same question.

Teachers Presentation: Structure and Procedure of the Theme Work

The following is a summary of the teachers' presentation of the project work. There is first of all a description of the common introduction, then a series of social science sessions and the parallel natural science sessions and finally, the conclusion.

The Common Introduction

The project was introduced with a dramatisation of a news broadcast performed by the teachers. The news items concerned consumption and climate change and had the following headlines: Record Christmas Shopping Statistics; Typhoon Devastates South Pacific Island; Indian Cold Snap; Swedish Cows Producing Less Milk; New Year's Eve Celebrations Marred By Violence and Doping Scandal In Spanish League. The details of the headlines were not included in the dramatisation, as the main aim was to capture the interest of the students and to stimulate some thought in the initial stage of the project. The students were also given the criteria explaining how the project work would be assessed.

Lesson Series in Social Studies

Lesson 1 – Consumption: We started with students' own consumption habits: What decisions do we make when we select a product? What are the deciding factors involved when we purchase e.g. food and clothes? Students first discussed this in pairs/groups and then later the whole group exchanged their views and information, and the results were drawn up in a mind map on the white board. Included in the mind map were points such as: price, label, appearance, taste, quality, environmental friendliness and habits. The discussion extended to deciding on the aspect which carried most importance in purchasing a product. The students were given a follow up assignment as homework, which involved interviewing three people and gathering similar information about their consumer habits.

Lesson 2 – Consumption and advertising: We began this section by filling in the mind map with the results of the students' interviews and a discussion was started based on the topic of the different types of environmentally friendly labelling e.g. the dolphin design on dolphin friendly tuna. The discussion progressed to advertising: In what ways does advertising influence us? What factors determine whether an advertisement is good or not? The discussion also included the various techniques applied by retailers in an attempt to make us buy more e.g. multi-packs, impulse purchases close to the checkout, appealing music, lighting, advertised products strategically placed at the back of the shop, hand-written price labels and using 9's on all price tags. The students' homework was to read a text in preparation for the following four-stage assignment: 'Refrigerators in China'. Here students were given the task of taking a standpoint on either who should be responsible for reducing/stopping the sale of refrigerators which release chlorofluorocarbons into the atmosphere, or whether the student feels what goes on in China is not an issue in Europe. Four alternatives to this situation were presented as a stimulus for a discussion on the conflicting opinions between an environmentalist viewpoint, a social/societal viewpoint and an economic viewpoint. The alternatives are A) We should not allow the Chinese to purchase this type of refrigerator B) Sell European refrigerators at a low cost C) We should be involved in ensuring that all refrigerators in China are environmentally friendly D) We should not be concerned with refrigerators in China. The homework assignment was for the students to read through the four alternatives and decide which statement they agreed with the most (they was also required to defend their standpoint in the discussion group during the next lesson).

Lesson 3 – Consumer patterns: The discussion following the homework assignment was lively, with a great deal of questioning and debating. This developed into discussions on what people actually need for survival. Do we really need refrigerators? What would happen during a sustained power cut? Would we survive?

Lesson 4 – Differences in standard of living between industrial countries and developing countries: We discussed different consumption habits in various countries and how the consumption patterns of food and energy in particular varied in different parts of the world. The stu-

216

dents raised the question concerning possible ways of a more equal method of resource distribution and this developed into speculation on what they themselves were prepared to give up in their own lives to benefit this idea. The students were asked how they felt a country's level of development or standard of welfare should be measured. Suggestions included not only the economic situation in a country, but also aspects such as literacy, infant mortality, education standards, daily calorific intake and equality. The discussion also included the terms GNP and HDI. The homework assignment was to read two depictions of future scenarios, one utopian the other dystopian, written from an environmental and population point of view. The reading exercise was followed by a written exercise in which students chose the depiction they found most realistic and gave reasons for their choice.

Lesson 5 –The Rio conference: We began with a short discussion on the homework assignment and continued to address the decisions reached during the Rio conference in 1992, as well as how the interests and viewpoints of different groups or countries can come into conflict with each other. Homework: How should the developing countries act when faced with the choice of obtaining food and basic survival needs or caring for the local and global environment?

Lessons 6, 7, 8 – Role-play: The feedback from the homework assignment resulted in another lively discussion. A role-play was initiated on the subject of a United Nations crisis meeting in Geneva concerning a new genetically modified cereal in connection with a violent uprising in El Dorado (fictional country). El Dorado has been regularly importing cheap cereal products from EU surpluses and has stopped domestic production as a consequence and started producing a luxury export crop e.g. coffee. However, this year, the EU's genetically modified crop has been devastated by parasites and the remaining cereal is now very highly priced. A result of this is that El Dorado cannot afford the new prices and a food shortage breaks out which also triggers violent acts among university students. The participants in the role-play are students in El Dorado, the director of the company 'FOOD 4 U', trade experts from the WTO, the Foreign Minister of El Dorado, farmers in both Sweden and El Dorado, the Swedish Ambassador to El Dorado and Swedish students. The class was divided into eight groups each group receiving a card indicating the role they are to play. The groups were also given a brief explanation about their potential opponents and partners, in addition to an overview of the entire area of dispute. The teachers assumed the role of leaders and made sure the proceedings kept moving, as well as informing the whole group of the international community's reactions to the events. The main objective was that the whole group reached some sort of compromise. Many different opinions and standpoints were aired during the exercise and the players had to form their own positions on the situation. Lessons 6 and 7 were allocated for all the necessary preparation work before the role-play exercise (see further lesson 16–18 in natural sciences).

Lesson Series in the Natural Sciences

Lesson 1 – Lifecycle analysis: In pairs, students received the task of making an analysis of the lifecycles of two products: a loaf of bread and a plastic cup, a pair of jeans and an aluminium can, a woollen sweater and a candle, a carton of fruit juice and a glass jar, a fleece (sweater) and a newspaper, a packet of coffee and a steel saucepan or a wooden stool and a plastic carrier bag. The questions they were given were: What are the necessary raw materials for production? What else is required in addition to raw materials in the production process? What happens to the product when it is no longer needed? How do the production, utilisation and the discarding of these products affect the environment?

Lesson 2 – Where are the raw materials from? After the presentations of their lifecycle analyses, there was a short summary on the origins of the necessary raw materials required for these products: the plant kingdom, the animal kingdom and the earth (oil, minerals etc.) and it was also established that these are the only resources available to us. At the end of the lesson the students were encouraged to think about how they make choices when purchasing items and if there are alternative ways of making choices open to people e.g. young, old, rich, poor, fatigued, active, stressed families, single people etc. The homework assignment was to interview three people, preferably different ages, about how they choose (see lesson 1 in social studies series).

Lesson 3 – Consumption habits and their influences on the greenhouse effect: The lesson began with feedback and discussions based on the homework assignment. We also discussed the role of advertising in consumer habits (see social sciences lesson 3). This was followed by an illustration of the connection between their lifecycle analyses in lesson 1 and the carbon dioxide and other greenhouse gas emissions that are the result of the production and transportation processes. There was a repetition of the details of the greenhouse effect.

Lesson 4, 5 – Energy sources: the advantages and disadvantages: With the help of their lifecycle analyses, students studied the advantages and disadvantages of various energy sources.

Lesson 6, 7 – Energy consumption in the production and distribution of commodities: Students investigated how certain similar products can effect the environment differently. Everybody received a handout showing a comparison between two types of potato chips. The main focus was on the amount of raw materials involved in the production, as well as the amount of energy that was used. The group decided that differences could depend on: different ways of packaging, the varying amount of stages in production and transportation distances. The homework was to think of other products which would produce the same types of contrasts as the potato chips. In the following feedback session students suggested: concentrated products compared with diluted (e.g. juices, detergents etc.), refill products (jam etc.) raw ingredients compared with semi-manufactured products etc. We made a short summary of how the production and transportation processes affect the environment. In addition to the raw materials, energy consumption is determined by the number of stages in the production process, how advanced the packaging is, how much transportation is involved (this depends on the location of the raw materials, where the product is made and how much space the product takes up in shipments etc.).

Lesson 8 – Fair trade labelling: After watching a film on coffee production, we discussed fair trade issues and why it is possible to say that a cup of coffee is 'too cheap'.

Lesson 9 – Production and energy consumption: We revised the material we had previously covered concerning production, although here the focus was on raw materials in the form of fruit and vegetables. Students answered the following questions using reference material and also relying on their own knowledge of the subject: A) Many of the commodities we consume come from the vegetable kingdom, the food we eat for example, but other products are also included. What are these other commodities from the vegetable kingdom that are not food products? B) If a farmer wants the best crop results from his land what steps does he/she take? C) Almost every form of cultivation affects the immediate environment in one way or another. How?

Lesson 10 – Biological diversity and moral choice: We went through the questions raised in lesson nine and students presented their findings to the group. Afterwards the group saw a film on bio diversity and the following questions were issued at the end of it. A) What is biological diversity? B) Which reasons were given in the film for maintaining the present biological diversity C) Do you think that there are species of plant or animal which are more important or should be more highly valued than others? Give reasons for your choice/s. D) Do you think that a species should be protected just because humans benefit from it or do they have a right to live independently of humans? These questions were discussed within the group; there were many differing opinions, particularly on the matter of some species having more value than others. Some thought that some species are unnecessary e.g. tics. The discussion developed into the dependency relationships between the species and the fact that it is almost impossible to predict what will be of use in the future. Some of the students were of the opinion that all the species share equal value, while others thought that humans held a superior position in the world; these statements led to a heated debate on the issues at hand.

Lesson 12 – Repetition: The group read a report on how various different treatments of the same raw material (a carrot) can lead to significant changes in energy consumption. We also compared different ways of using 100 kg peas, and how much food can be derived from them if they are eaten as they are in comparison to being used as a food source for other animals.

Lesson 13, 14 – A question of responsibility in terms of environmental influence: The group watched a TV programme which addressed the production of two relatively obscure commodities: palm oil from Indonesia and soja beans from Brazil, and how the production of these commodities affects the host countries as well as how EU agricultural policies affect the rest of the world etc. In the ensuing discussion, the focus was on pinning down where the responsibility lay in the destruction of the rich tropical rain forests of Indonesia and Brazil in order to enable the production of palm oil and soja beans. This was followed by a four-point exercise (see social sciences lesson 2). The question was, who is responsible for the destruction of the rain forests? The alternatives given were: the consumers who buy the products, the politicians, the middlemen or the corporations who grow the palms or soja beans. The students chose whichever alternative suited them best and then gave reasons for their choices and questioned the choices of other students. The discussion was consolidated by students writing a report on the subject in which they also defended their standpoints. There was an additional discussion on whether or not it is acceptable to invest money in companies that make profits as a result of densely populated environments being destroyed for production purposes; and why the EU has such high revenues on the import of food products but not on the import of animal feed, and the effects this has on the choice of crop cultivation in countries outside the EU.

Lesson 15 – Preparation for role-play: See SS lesson 6–8.

Lesson 16, 17, 18 – Role-play: The final lesson began with students changing into costume; they received nametags as well as props to be used in their respective roles. The classroom was furnished to resemble a conference room with the tables in a U shape and a large UN flag at the front. The conference was facilitated by two teachers, who made sure that all the delegates had a say in the issues. The objective was that they should all reach an agreement as regards a suitable solution to the problem. The conference began with each of the delegates presenting themselves and their viewpoint on the problem, after which the floor was open for debate. After approx. 30 minutes of activity, the debate was stopped for a short break and an opportunity was given for individual delegates to confer with any potential partners. Following this, groups presented new solutions which included various proposals towards compromises.

Examples of the proposals included the EU promising to lower their subsidies to farmers to allow for more competition in the agricultural market; the WTO allowed a non EU country to introduce import duties on food in order for the country to change its crops from animal feed to food products, and in addition the World Bank would either drop the country's debt or repayment would be deferred until the country's economic situation had improved. Discussions followed the conference for 30 minutes.

Test: The students sat a test which comprised of an evaluation of the knowledge gained during the entire project.

Conclusion: Teaching Competence in Education for Sustainable Development

We pointed out in the introduction that, in order to effectively teach sustainable development, it was necessary to integrate the three following components: (i) knowledge of environmental problems and sustainable development; (ii) theoretical knowledge of teaching and learning; and (iii) practical knowledge and teaching skills (teaching experience). In the first part of this conclusion we will present an overview of how this level of competence can be achieved. This will be followed by a summary of the central areas of knowledge and experience within education for sustainable development which this book has provided.

In the introduction, a schematic diagram was presented to describe the layout of the book. The same diagram can also be used to describe how teaching competence within sustainable development can be acquired.

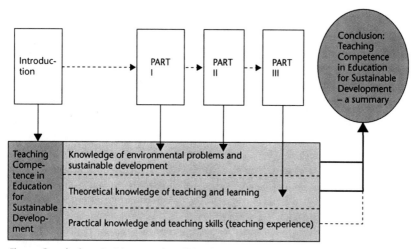

Figure Conclusion: 1. Diagram describing how teaching competence within sustainable development can be acquired.

In broad terms, Parts I and II addressed different aspects of environmental knowledge and different perspectives on environmental issues: environmental history, human ecology and human geography; ecology, environmental ethics, sociology and economy respectively. Many other areas of knowledge could, of course, be added to this list, e.g. political science, environmental law, physical geography and chemistry. The main reason for the choices made is due to the specific contributions that we feel those perspectives make towards the line of reasoning supported by education for sustainable development (see Part III).

Part I explained how the relationship between societies and the natural world is changeable, and how this implies that a person's recognition of this fact is a product of the learning experience. In Part III, this aspect received further study and the teaching and learning perspectives were underlined as being the main perspectives.

A central message in Part II is that environmental issues cannot be simply reduced to a matter of knowledge and information. Equally important elements in these issues are the environmentally ethical standpoints of individuals, as well as the political and democratic content of our attempts to create collective guidelines on how we should relate to the natural world and the issues surrounding environmental damage. This broad perspective on environmental issues was used in Part III in the presentation of different procedures in learning knowledge and morals in schools. Here, it was also possible to demonstrate the associations between the process of learning knowledge and the process of learning opinions, attitudes and values. The above procedure indicates that, based on the book's structure, forming teaching competence in education for sustainable development requires both knowledge and experience of practical teaching, in addition to theoretical knowledge of sustainable development. Part III was concluded with a number of practical examples of education for sustainable development, which illustrate how these components can be interrelated.

Education for Sustainable Development: A Summary

If we focus on the main starting point in education for sustainable development, from which it is understood that students are to develop a critically reflective relationship towards society's environmental and developmental issues, it is vitally important to consider how this can effectively be achieved in the teaching and learning process. Below is a summarised presentation of the book's most important content, which we hope, in addition to the teaching examples in chapter twelve, will be found useful.

Perspectives on Environmental and Developmental Issues

The book begins with an historical overview of humankind's relationship with its environment; our initial interest was in the distinction between whether or not humans were just another species of the animal kingdom or whether they could be more closely linked with the term: cultural beings. We later followed how humankind has successively developed ever increasing and complex technological methods of utilising the natural world. We started with the hunter-collector period, their basic tools and weapons, their knowledge of the environment and their social cohesion; all of which enabled them to hunt and kill animals which were vastly superior to them in size and strength. We then looked at agricultural developments such as the plough, draught animals, storage and drainage techniques, when it became possible to produce much larger amounts of food, and as a consequence sustain a larger group of people from the same area of land. Our final focus was on transnational corporations and global markets, where all forms of production, from garden chairs and loaves of bread to office complexes and computer equipment, is the main priority.

In chapters two and three we drew attention towards the ongoing discussions that address the question of humans' place in the natural world and the fact that these types of outlook have always kept pace with technological development. Is humankind able to continue to develop increasingly complex systems indefinitely? Is our increased distance from natural environments also a measure of our distance from human values? In this section we also paid particular attention to the development of modern environmental commitment during the 20th Century, from nature conservation to environmental protection and ultimately, sustainable development. In addition to this we highlighted a handful of central themes in contemporary environmental and natural resource discussions. These included how environmental issues have become more abstract, global and diffuse at the same time as being closely linked to individual consumption habits and lifestyles. We also underlined the increased ethical relevance involved in issues concerning the environment and natural resources. The sciences, natural and social, can only contribute to a certain point towards determining a reasonable and right way to deal with questions about natural resources, the developing countries and the future. These questions must all also be discussed from ideological and existential perspectives. Part I was concluded with both the challenge and the opportunities which lie in an increasing awareness for outdoor recreation and 'green' social planning as a means of transcending what was referred to as an 'instant society within walls' in which we live today.

Part II began by approaching environmental problems as knowledge-based issues; the main focus was on an ecological understanding of the natural world. The natural sciences, not least ecology, have had a great deal of influence on the discovery and our understanding of the environmental hazards created by modern society. And even though there seems to be a general consensus within the scientific community concerning the 'big picture' of the environmental situation, there are still differing opinions on the vulnerability of the natural world and the significance of human interaction.

In chapter five environmental problems were defined as being changes in the natural world caused by our exploitation of it, which has resulted in the creation of a conflict of values and interests. In the process of interpreting and implementing scientific findings in our daily lives or in planning social development strategies, values are always a crucial element. When we make judgements about how to relate to the natural world and environmental issues, we are also forming individual environmental morals. The conscious and systematic reflection on the basis and motives for environmental moral judgements we termed environmental ethics. In chapter five we were able to state that there are many lines of reasoning regarding how we should see human relationship to nature and how we should interact with the natural world and the environment.

As a society we are faced with the challenge of coordinating these lines of reasoning into collective decisions which address how society should relate to the natural world, solve environmental problems, distribute natural resources etc. All these decisions are of crucial importance for the development of today's society and the realisation of a future society. Our collective choices on how to approach environmental issues will, therefore, have an effect on the opportunities and limitations of individuals within society. This allowed us, in chapter six, to draw the conclusion that, to a great extent, environmental issues are also political issues. The need for cooperation between politics and science when forming strategies for sustainable development was further corroborated in chapter seven, where economics, in particular environmental economics, was introduced into the discussion.

Late and post-modernists point towards a cultural development during the last decades to illustrate an increased questioning of established authorities and traditions and also the fact that previously accepted social values and objectives are no longer automatically observed. Particularly in post-modern opinion, there seems to be a strong scepticism towards universally accepted knowledge, e.g. knowledge which claims to understand 'the essence of reality'. The idea that the scientific community should be the sole representatives of 'the truth' has therefore been contested. Regardless of how closely one is associated with these types of post-modern discussions, in our globalised and diverse community – which is in great need of a more sustainable development plan – there is every reason to not automatically accept the political, scientific and economic ground rules that for so long have been the building blocks of modern industrial societies. The resulting pluralism of this approach makes the democratic aspects of our ways of managing environmental and developmental problems much more apparent.

Perspectives on the Processes of Learning and Teaching

In Part III, we shifted our line of reasoning to a school environment and we discussed the various implications of education for sustainable development (ESD). As a clarification of ESD, in chapter eight we compared the differences between ESD and other earlier selective traditions within environmental education in schools. In the light of the comparisons it could be seen that the specific characteristics of ESD advocated a broader scope, both in time and space, a more detailed perspective on conflicting viewpoints and a closer relationhipe to ethical and political perspectives. This indicates that a central aim of this tradition is to create citizens who have the ability to critically evaluate the alternative perspectives on environmental and developmental problems.

To be able to evaluate ESD in relation to the other traditions within environmental education, in chapter nine we turned to the democratic elements of education as a common point of reference. Here we addressed two objectives of democracy in schools: (i) teaching should be based on participation in decision-making; (ii) students are to become knowledgeable citizens who actively partake in environmental debates in society. We attempted to demonstrate, in the realisation of these two objectives, that it is important to be aware how environmental and developmental questions are presented, as this have an effect on what students learn both about their role and status in the classroom (participation) and how they see themselves as citizens. Accordingly, democratic ideals are continuously present during lessons.

The value comparisons which were made demonstrated that whilst other traditions within environmental education presuppose that the democratic process is something which is instilled either *before* or *after* the teaching/learning process, in ESD the democratic process is integrated *in* the education itself. This suggests that critical discussions on topics such as different alternatives and their consequences are an essential part of education itself and that ESD accordingly has a great opportunity, compared with other traditions, to live up to the democratic objectives of schools.

In chapters ten and eleven, we made a closer study of the ESD perspective by initially establishing a theoretical perspective on

228

learning, and later we discussed what it could mean to teach sustainable development based on the number of the choices that a teacher must make during a practical teaching situation.

It was our intention to point out that the learning of knowledge and morals can be understood in terms of creating new differences and similarities in relation to our previous experiences (chapter ten). The creation of these differences and similarities takes place in encounters between people or between individuals and their environment. Thus, learning always includes an individual's previous experiences, as well as what is taking place in a specific encounter.

Learning morals includes many different things. It can be a case of learning social rules (norms) which state the right and wrong approaches respectively of how to interact with other humans and the natural world. These norms are often linked with specific practices. Making moral judgements and knowing when it is relevant to pass such judgement is also something which is learnt. Learning to distinguish between social norms and personal convictions often happens in those situations when making these distinctions is necessary. Morals do not only appear in contexts of right and wrong, but are also present in encounters between individuals and individuals and their surroundings; which provides an opportunity to discuss these situations in terms of closed or open encounters. When we have understood the various situations in which morals play a daily role in our lives, we can begin to reflect on situations ethically: critically reviewing norms, our habits and behaviour during encounters etc. Environmentally ethical reflection is always characterised by the evaluation of alternatives, and this type of evaluation requires some system of measurement e.g. a benchmark. In order for students to be able to develop a reflective, environmentally ethical approach in relating to the world, they should be given the opportunity to critically evaluate and discuss the different ways of determining the benchmarks.

Values and attitudes are also assimilated into the learning process. We attempted to illustrate this by highlighting the criteria involved in the process of researching and describing the natural world from a scientific perspective. The criterion in question was the view of the natural world as a material object. This view can be referred to as a *companion meaning:* a viewpoint that is a consequence of having learnt something else (in this case scientific knowledge). If it is the case that all education involves companion meanings then it becomes central to ESD that students are allowed the opportunity to discuss and evaluate these. This is particularly clear when seen against the background of the fact that many moral debates are the result of people bringing attention to attitudes and values which are taken for granted within a social practice or an organization.

In chapter eleven, it was our aim, based on this line of reasoning within learning theory, to present a number of tools and models which can be used by teachers in the planning and discussion stages of ESD. The main point of the chapter was based on the basic choices a teacher makes in their professions: the choice of objectives and the reasons for those objectives, the choice of content, and the choice of forms and methods. In this chapter we tried to demonstrate how a democratic and pluralistic approach towards ESD has an effect on the above choices. An essential element was that more than one perspective on the problem or issue being addressed in the classroom is discussed, that the various alternatives are open to critical review, and that the students have the opportunity to experience democratic processes in practice. We also noted the importance of creating a balance between different types of encounter in which learning can take place: open and closed encounters respectively, and direct and indirect encounters respectively.

In chapter twelve we presented three teaching models which can be used in ESD. These models are a result of an integration of theoretical knowledge of environmental problems and sustainable development, theoretical knowledge of teaching and learning, and teaching experience. The models can therefore be perceived as illustrating the main idea in this book, namely that the integration of these three components is fruitful for developing the teaching competence within sustainable development.

An Educational Model for the Application of ESD

In the following we will summarise the chapters in part III in the form of an educational model that can be applicable in planning individual lessons and also in creating opportunities for discussions with colleagues (see fig. Conclusion: 2). The model presents the central choices which we must make when attempting to actualise the objectives laid down in ESD.

The model explains the process from the general objectives within education to the actual learning process. The first step indicates that a transformation of the main *goal* of education for sustainable development – create citizens who can actively participate in democratic debates concerning environment and development – to more specific goals is necessary e.g. goals which illustrate the reasons of choice behind each particular lesson or work topic. How this transformation is to take place is dependent on the educational philosophy preferred by each teacher, as well as their view on the problems surrounding environmental and developmental issues. The next step concerns transforming the teaching objective to the choice of content respectively forms and methods.

Choice of *content* is a matter of selecting the type of knowledge to be prioritised, in addition to choosing the moral approaches which are to be objects for discussion in the classroom. We have already stated the necessity of involving a democratic perspective in teaching for sustainable development combined with a pluralistic approach in these choices. We have even underlined that companion meanings are learnt as a result of studying a particular area or topic, i.e. discovering new ways of seeing and interacting with the world. These aspects require careful deliberation when choosing lesson content.

The choice of content must also be coordinated with the choice of teaching forms and methods i.e. the choice of the various encounters which students will partake in during lessons. Even in the choice of encounters the democratic perspective in education for sustainable development has all-inclusive consequences. A central aspect which was accentuated is that the students are given the opportunity to 'live through' democracy in these encounters. This implies that ESD should maintain a balance between the choices of *indirect* and *closed* encounters, in which, by using e.g. textbooks and attending lessons/lectures, students encounter knowledge and perspectives regarded as being central to our culture – and *direct* and *open* encounters, where students are given the opportunity to form their own understandings and, by means of ethical reflection, are able to critically evaluate the available alternatives.

To ensure that the education will be beneficial to students, it is important that both the choice of content and the teaching approach take the preferences of the students into consideration. It is also important that these choices are made in relation to the students' previous knowledge and experience, as well as allowing them opportunities to draw on these resources. If not, there is a risk that what is learnt during lessons will only be valid in the classroom and of no relevance for the students' life and actions outside school.

The results of the choices of teaching can affect the students' learning process in a variety of different ways. These include the type of knowledge and perspectives within sustainable development which the students develop; the moral standpoints which students adopt in environmental and developmental issues; the students' ability to make ethical evaluations, as well as their understanding of who has the right to make decisions in the classroom and even in society itself, i.e. the students' future role in democratic processes.

Research has shown that teachers' own experience as students has a great impact on the way they effectuate their own teaching. This indicates that there is a tendency among teachers to think that they have a general idea of what constitutes the correct way of teaching about environmental and developmental issues.

If there is no opportunity to distance ourselves, as teachers, from this preconceived notion and to recognise that there are other possible ways of conducting education for sustainable development, there is an increased risk of continuing to think that there is only one way of teaching. This can affect the credibility of what is being taught, i.e. there will be no way of convincingly justifying the educational approach we have chosen. Even a situation in which a teacher is aware that there are a number of other ways to approach education for sustainable development and yet still continues with his/her original method is preferable, as the knowledge of the existence of other approaches allows for the development of a line of reasoning that supports the original choice in favour of the alternatives. This type of awareness is important if we are to develop our own ways of teaching and how to co-operate, by means of constructive discussions and open attitudes with our colleagues. Any

232

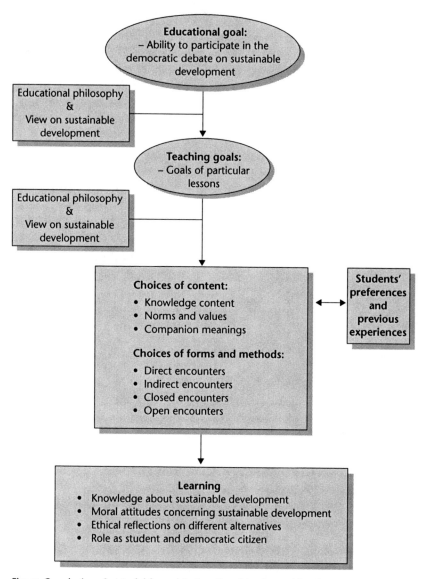

Figure Conclusion: 2. Model for achieving the objectives with education for sustainable development.

attempts to adhere to one approach will result in difficulties in discussing and understanding the opinions and standpoints of others. The above diagram can be used for reflecting on, or discussing, different aspects of education for sustainable development. In addition, it obliges us to actualise the central elements in which important choices are made as well as to take standpoints in educational philosophy questions which are, in turn, crucial to the outcome of the decision making process.

However, practical teaching experience is a central element in creating high levels of competence in teaching. By adding the practical knowledge of different teachers, e.g. about recognizing the importance of the students' social background, organising teamwork and the ability to identify what students feel would be both relevant and exciting components of the lessons, the model presented above can allow for the creation of a good level of competence within the teaching-staff in the teaching of education for sustainable development

Conclusions for Discussion within Education for Sustainable Development

The following is a summary of the book in the form of conclusions which can form the basis of a discussion or simply statements that individuals can form standpoints on. To ensure that a discussion or individual evaluation will contribute to an increased level of teaching competence, it is important that time is allowed for reflection on the reasons for our individual standpoints.

Based on the content of this book, we suggest that the following conclusions can be drawn:

- the relationship between human beings and the natural world has varied throughout history, but has always been a central element in our hopes, fears and future outlooks;
- in many ways human beings have successively detached themselves from the natural world both physically and intellectually, and one of the remaining few instances where humans, in modern industrial societies, have a concrete sense of contact with ecological cycles is in connection with out-of-doors;

- the problems surrounding our interrelation with the environment can be understood from several scientific perspectives;
- our interpretations and ways of relating to environmental problems are vital aspects in social development, as ultimately it is a matter of which type of future society we want to create;
- environmental problems are matters which concern knowledge and information as well as conflicts of values and viewpoints;
- the issue of environmental problems is, to the very greatest extent, a democratic issue;
- teachers do not have the right to decide the correct ways of evaluation (if education is to be democratic each person must be permitted to choose his/her individual standpoint);
- an environmentally moral as well as a democratic dimension is always present during teaching on the environment and sustainable development;
- learning that takes place in open and direct encounters has moral and democratic implications different to learning which take place in closed and indirect encounters;
- a central element in education is that students are given the opportunity to conduct ethical discussions based on the theoretical knowledge, companion meanings and environmentally moral approaches they have encountered during lessons;
- it is important that students are allowed to practice the critical evaluation (ethical and knowledge based) of different alternatives and as a consequence develop the ability to participate in democratic debates on the environment;
- it is important that students are given time to understand, discuss and evaluate social conflicts that touch on environmental and developmental issues;
- it is important that students are given the opportunity to 'live through' democracy during the lessons; and
- it is important that students are given opportunities to experience conflicts between different interests in environmental and developmental issues (in the capacity of both individuals and citizens) e.g. by participation in role-plays.

The Authors

Klas Sandell is a senior lecturer in human geography, has a Ph.D. and is an associate professor. The main areas of his work are in research and teaching in environmental history and human ecology and he is involved in various scientific research programs, e.g.: 'Landscape as Arena: Science, Institutions and the Discourses on Environment, 1800–2000' and 'The Mountain Mistra Programme'. He is currently associated with the Research Unit for Tourism and Leisure and the Department of Geography and Tourism at the University of Karlstad, Sweden. Apart from working on a number of scientific projects on human ecology, the history of 'outdoor life', the right of public access and the interaction between contact with nature and environmental commitment, Klas Sandell has, in addition to a number of scientific texts, been the author of popular science books such as Friluftslivets pedagogik (Teaching on outdoor life; Eds. Brügge, Glantz & Sandell, Liber 2002, second edition) and Friluftshistoria (The history of outdoor life in Sweden; Eds. Sandell & Sörlin, Carlssons 2000).

Johan Öhman is a university lecturer at the department of Physical Education and Health at Örebro University, Sweden, and has for a number of years taught human ecology, outdoor life, and environmental education. In addition to this he has also been involved in continuation courses for teachers. His area of research is in environmental morals and democratic issues within the sphere of education for sustainable development. He has been responsible for many assignments and commissions on behalf of the Swedish National Agency of Education and the Swedish National Agency for School Improvement. He has written and co-written a number of articles and texts on environmental and sustainable education, and has also been editor of the anthology: Learning to Change Our

World? : Swedish research on education & sustainable development (Eds. Wickenberg, Axelsson, Frizén, Helldén & Öhman, Studentlitteratur, 2004).

Leif Östman is a senior lecturer in education at the Department of Teacher Training at Uppsala University, Sweden. He has a Ph.D. and is an associate professor. He is educated as a lower secondary school teacher in the subjects of Biology, Chemistry and Geography, although for many years he has taught teacher students and research students in courses relating to socio cultural perspectives on learning, science education and environmental education. He heads the research group SMED (Studies of Meaning in Educational Discourses); he also is the leading figure for a number of projects involving environmental education as well as being responsible for several development and research projects, commissioned by government departments, within the same field. In addition to a number of scientific articles, he has also authored: Problems of Meaning in Science Curriculum (Eds. Roberts & Östman: Teachers College Press, 1998) and Textanalys (Text analyses; Eds. Säfström & Östman, Studentlitteratur, 1999).

Index